No Price I Bring

To Randy & Drepel —

Joel Cooper

No Price I Bring

Joel Cooper

iUniverse, Inc.
New York Lincoln Shanghai

No Price I Bring

iUniverse books may be ordered through booksellers or by contacting:

iUniverse
2021 Pine Lake Road, Suite 100
Lincoln, NE 68512
www.iuniverse.com
1-800-Authors (1-800-288-4677)

Because of the dynamic nature of the Internet, any Web addresses or links contained in this book may have changed since publication and may no longer be valid.

The views expressed in this work are solely those of the author and do not necessarily reflect the views of the publisher, and the publisher hereby disclaims any responsibility for them.

ISBN: 978-0-595-48427-0 (pbk)
ISBN: 978-0-595-60518-7 (ebk)

Printed in the United States of America

To
Bill and the Boys

Contents

Acknowledgments

Ann Davis read the manuscript and made the necessary changes in punctuation, grammar, spelling, and sentence structure.
Thanks, Ann

Wm. Christopher Cooper did the formatting.
Thanks, Son

Word Perfect's Spell Checker and Grammatix did it's usual good job.

Before You Start Reading this Book

This book is a deliberate mixture of fact and fiction written in this form to satisfy: (1) my attempt to be honest, (2) my hope to tell an interesting story with a point, and (3) my earnest desire to protect those with whom I have interacted (and myself) for these three score years and ten plus.

About <u>honesty:</u> Since I am telling you from the beginning that this book is both reality and fantasy, I will not have to try so hard (as I write) to make certain that everything is the "gospel truth." If I were writing biography, I would feel obligated to try to present the unvarnished story—an impossible assignment for me, maybe for anybody. Nevertheless, writing fact/fiction means that I am "freed up," relieved of the anxiety about being honest.

Moreover, I am skeptical about anyone being able to write accurate personal history. Much of what parades as fact is fact/fiction at best and fiction in disguise at worst. I can say with fair accuracy what is pure fabrication in this story, but I am not so certain about that which is fact. Memory, for one thing, plays all sorts of tricks on me. While I can remember WHAT happened, I will be opinionated about WHY it happened. Moreover, I will probably be mistaken about my dominant motives and reactions at the time. So when I am dealing in this fact/fiction book with what I perceive to be a true experience, I will feel no necessity to "tell the truth, the whole truth, and nothing but the truth."

About <u>telling an interesting story with a point</u>: Frankly, I want to tell an interesting story, because I want someone to read it. Would you fault me for that? Also, I want to make a point, because that is what I have been trying to do all my professional life. This may sound dreadfully "dated," reminiscent of days when a story had a discernable moral. If so, let it be. I join Pilate in saying, "What I have written, I have written." However, it may just be that some literati are waiting for a return of such a story. If you think I am going to tell you in this introduction what lesson is to be found in these pages, you are mistaken. That mistake would be like a mystery writer telling you "who done it" before the story begins. However, I will not try to conceal the point until the last moment, Agatha. I hope you readers would experience dawning as you read.

In a sense the introduction of any fictitious material into the factual account converts the whole into fiction. Yet, fiction can become truth, i.e., when the fictitious makes a point that is true. This I hope to do, or I have fumbled the ball and the other side has recovered it.

About <u>my desire to protect those with whom I have interacted</u>: My family and friends will, no doubt, want me to delineate that which is fact. I can hear them now, "Did that really happen?" Since I have already shown the difficulty of answering, I will keep my peace—for now, at least, which at my age may be forever. All who enjoy fantasizing, if they wish, may see themselves or me somewhere in the story. I have not changed all names "to protect the innocent" or the guilty. Yet when the use of a real name might bring embarrassment to someone or litigation to me, I have changed the name or not used one.

Finally, this fact/fiction approach may put a safety net under me, if someone should challenge my presentation of the "facts" or think I have slandered them.

—Joel Cooper, September 2006.

1

Poison Pen

The letter read: "What a sad mistake if you help elect Joel Cooper bishop. He is not what the church needs today! He has let his local church suffer all these many years while he ran for bishop. He is not a dynamic leader. His ego has been in his way many years."

I will not defend myself against the accusations which the poison pen letter describes so clearly. They may be true—to some extent. The motivations and feelings which I had about becoming a bishop in the United Methodist Church were so complex that they stubbornly resisted my best effort to sort them out. Why *did* I want to be a bishop? I am certain only of this: I had mixed motives. At the very worst: ego; at the very best: the conviction that God was *calling* me to the office. Somewhere between was the Truth, but I did not know where it was then, nor do I know now.

Even if the writer spoke some truth in the letter, I did not feel it was the proper way to work against my election to the episcopacy. (As I read again the previous sentence, I acknowledge that it is a vast *understatement* of my feelings). What really motivated such a letter at a time when I was considered a viable candidate for election? I suspected that it was a revenge attempt by someone who perceived that I had wronged them, probably someone from Central U.M.C., Fayetteville. If I had wronged someone, it could have been unwittingly or deliberately—although the second is more difficult for me to admit. Someone chose the poison pen as the way to get even with me. Of course, this does not mean that he\she did not really believe what he/she had written. I fault the poison penner, not for insincerity, nor for an absolute falsehood, but for unethical political methodology amounting to a heinous act in any civilized culture. In short, it was just tacky.

If by chance the author of the letter should be reading this, I want you to know that I have worked thru this matter. If it didn't sound so pious, I would say that I have forgiven you. In any event forgiving you is what I have tried to do. As it turned out, I don't think the letters had a significant impact on my failure to be elected. That helps me in my struggle to forgive you, although you may be disappointed that you largely wasted your efforts. However, you surely must have enjoyed my defeat in the episcopal elections. One other thing: I think I know the identity of the person who wrote the letters. If, guilty one, you are reading this, you will continue wondering if I know it is you.

During Bishop's Week on Mt. Sequoyah, someone distributed several copies of the poison pen letter to the bishops and some delegates to the Jurisdictional Conference. The postmark was "Fayetteville" on the envelope containing the copy of the letter sent to Buddy Arnold, a lay delegate. A typewriter with clear type characteristics addressed the envelope. I could have matched this printing easily with the typewriter of my suspect, but that action could have brought great embarrassment to innocent people. Moreover, what if my suspect had been completely innocent? They scrawled the letter itself in large letters, a deliberate effort to make the tracing of the handwriting difficult. They then made copies of poor quality on a copying machine. I still have the letter and envelop in my file, although I do not think of them as "treasured keepsakes."

To be "in the running" for the episcopacy is a heady thing. United Methodist bishops have power, prestige, and permanency. For me to say that these rewards were not involved in my "run" for the episcopacy is probably a lie.

Bishops have the power to appoint pastors to churches. This appointive power spills over into many other areas, which may be good or bad depending upon the character of the bishop. So, the office of a bishop in the United Methodist Church is a position of real power over the lives of thousands.

Moreover, a bishop possesses prestige. The office of a bishop is a highly honored position in the United Methodist Church. This is not as true now in the 21st century as it has been. I do not feel that the dimunition of the episcopacy has resulted from the failure of the bishops. They have been able and effective, for the most part. "The times are a changin'. Monolithic structures of all kinds are under attack, but in 1980 a bishop was still "someone to look up to."

Moreover, a bishop is always a bishop, although he/she must retire at approximately 65 years of age. Being considered for the episcopacy by one's associates in the church, with the extra attention, accolades, and outright apple-polishing is enough to turn one's head. It is no wonder I have a crick in my neck from time to time.

It was the best of times; far from the worst. At least, this was true for me. The ecclesiastical judicatory to which I belonged, the North Arkansas Conference of the United Methodist Church, had nominated me for the episcopacy. The delegates from the North Arkansas Conference and the delegates from the Little Rock Annual Conference had agreed to support me in the elections which were to be held in July of 1980. Moreover, the jurisdictional conference which elects bishops was to meet in Little Rock, home ground, if you please, giving me some advantage, presumably. Since I had received considerable support in the voting of 1976, and many delegates knew me, I reasoned that I had a good chance to be elected, but never felt strongly that it would happen.

It was hot in Little Rock, Arkansas, on July 15, 1980, as the conference of the South Central Jurisdiction of the United Methodist Church began. From across the states of Nebraska, Kansas, Oklahoma, New Mexico (part), Texas, Louisiana, Arkansas, and Missouri, approximately 350 voting delegates had assembled for the main purpose of electing five new bishops to fill vacancies created by the retirement of five bishops. These new bishops and the ones still active would be assigned to the areas within the jurisdiction to serve in that area for the next quadrennium (four years), at least.

The delegates from the North Arkansas Conference were as follows: Chairman of the delegation Joel A. Cooper, Jim Beal, Charles E. Ramsay, Ben F. Jordan, Charles P. McDonald, Charles E. Casteel, William P. Connell, Earl B. Carter, William E. Arnold, Jr., Mrs. Emily Cockrill, Robert D. Cheyne, Euba Winton, Gene Brand, Marvin Gaither, Pat Freemeyer, Phyllis Hall Johnson, The alternates were: Robert E. Felder, Norman Carter, Ms. Marie T. Jordan, June Spotts. It was a splendid group. The delegation selected Jim Beal to lead the campaign to get me elected. I am uncomfortable with the term "campaign" with its overtones of political maneuvering, but I must record that everything was not left to Providence. My friends helped me put my best foot forward and to keep it out of my mouth, both difficult tasks. They raised some money to help with expenses. I never knew the amount nor the persons making contributions. It was more than adequate. Among other things, attractive brochures were distributed containing testimonials from various persons of prominence. These persons were: Roy B. Shilling, Jr, President of Hendrix College, Nell B. Barling, President of United Methodist Women, South Central Jurisdiction, the Hon. Dale Bumpers, United States Senator, J. Frank Broyles, Director of Athletics at the University of Arkansas, Mrs. Euba Winton, General Conference Lay Delegate, Bob Cheyne, Executive Committee United Methodist Communications. Of course, they tempt me to record what they said, but that strikes me as a bit unseemly. If I am pressed, I could produce a copy of the brochure.

At the General Conference which met in May of 1980 in Indianapolis, several delegations from the conferences receiving new bishops in September interrogated me. Naturally, the delegates wanted to know something about the "candidates," for somebody elected would be their own bishop. They asked me all sorts of questions, everything except, "What do you think about ordaining homosexuals?", a question which had not become an issue at that time. I answered the questions as best I could, trying to be honest, knowing I could not please everyone. The experience was somewhat like judging a show horse; i.e., the delegates wanted to find out if I had the "mane and tail" to be a bishop, or, to put it in a more sophisticated way, "did I fill out their created profile?" No one actually asked me to show my teeth, but I had the feeling that they were stealing a look when I grinned. I suppose this sort of "cat-scan" has its values, but it is a very trying experience for the "cat."

The northern states of the jurisdiction (Arkansas, Missouri, Nebraska, Kansas) had formed a loosely organized coalition to elect some bishops from that area. This organization was felt to be necessary, because of the voting strength of Texas and Oklahoma. Delegates generally conceded that any person backed by Oklahoma and Texas could be elected to the episcopacy.

The story of the balloting is full of "what if's", but I will not recount them. On the first ballot, with five bishops to be elected, I was seventh in the ranking, receiving 115 votes with 218 votes necessary for election. Not a very good start. No election. W.T. Handy from Louisiana was elected on the second ballot and I moved into fifth place with 148 votes. John Wesley Hardt from Texas was elected on the third ballot,.and I had dropped ten votes to 138. Bad sign. It was down hill for the next few ballots for me. Ben Oliphant from Texas was elected on the fifth ballot and Louis Schowengerdt from Missouri was elected on the sixth. That left one bishop to be elected, but that was not going to be easy. Bruce Blake, John Russell and Walter Underwood were "head to head" on ballot seven. On ballot nine John Russell of Oklahoma was only seventeen votes from election, but he dropped votes in the next four ballots. Bruce Blake received 158 votes in ballots eight, nine, and ten, and then started to drop. On the twelfth ballot Walter Underwood of Texas began to move up, but I had entered the picture again with 28 votes. It was then that the northern coalition decided to try again to elect me, and on the 13th ballot I received 139 votes to lead the group. There were caucuses after that. I am sure they involved Texas delegates and others. On the fourteenth ballot Walter Underwood had 163 votes to my 154. Ballot number fifteen resulted in 162 votes for Walter Underwood and 152 for me. On ballot sixteen I went ahead of Underwood 168 to 165. This was the highest number of votes I received, just 48 votes short of election. At this point, Bishop Kenneth Hicks of Arkansas thought I would be elected and he alerted Mrs. Hicks to be ready for the usual escort duties. After this, the delegates from the northern coalition decided that neither Underwood nor I could be elected and so turned to Bill McElvaney, who received 118 votes on the eighteenth ballot. However, Underwood continued to "hang in there." By now it was obvious that neither McElvaney nor Underwood could be elected, so the delegates turned back to John Russell who had received 24 votes on the nineteenth ballot, and gave him 135 votes on the 20th ballot. He was elected easily on ballot twenty two. That made five bishops elected to fill the vacancies. Walter Underwood and Bruce Blake would be elected in future jurisdictional conferences. I would never be a bishop. My Mama would be disappointed.

This balloting took place over a period of three days. I remember that I did not sleep one of those nights. My election was possible, but what was going to happen? I tried to tell myself that whatever happened would be all right, but the uncertainty and excitement of it all did not lull me to sleep. On the one hand, I wanted to be elected. On the other hand, I had fears that I would not make a good bishop, would be embarrassed by failures to serve effectively. And, as I have already said, I never had strong feelings that I would be elected. As I look back upon the experience today and see the problems which bishops face, I think that the Lord (and some interesting circumstances) may have saved me from a great deal of anguish, to a mostly pleasant ministry in Ft. Smith.

Bishop Hicks knew that I should move from Central United Methodist Church Fayetteville. There were some lay persons in Central, Fayetteville who felt that the church needed a change in pastors. I had been pastor there for thirteen years and three months, longer than any pastor before. They may have expressed to the bishop their wishes for a change, I do not know. But I agreed with them, I was ready to move and felt that my moving would be best for Central. Bishop Hicks was able to appoint me to First UMC, Ft. Smith, when George Ivy, the pastor there, indicated that he was ready to retire on September 1.

It would be interesting to know what went on behind the scenes in the caucusing at the Jurisdictional Conference. I don't criticize this "political maneuvering". Delegates have to get their heads together, if anyone is to be elected. Unfortunately, it sometimes boils down to the question, "Who *can* be elected?", rather than "Who *ought* to be elected." (I am not saying that **I** ought to have been elected.) Naturally, the conferences with the largest number of votes have the advantage. Someone, I am sure, is smart enough to come up with a system to elect our bishops which gives the smaller conferences a better chance to see one of their own elected.

In 1980 the North Arkansas Conference had never had one of its ministers elected to the episcopacy while serving in the conference. I am happy to report that this unfortunate record was broken at the Jurisdictional Conference of 2000 when Max Whitfield of the North Arkansas Conference was elected.

Years earlier Aubrey Walton was elected bishop while serving in Arkansas (Little Rock Conference). Several ministers, who started out in Arkansas but transferred to other conferences, have been elected. Among these are Paul Galloway and Kenneth Shamblin. There may be others.

Well, I had to preach a last sermon at Central. That was not going to be easy. I had been through difficult times with the members: two fires in the sanctuary, "hippy" days, the days of student unrest with its attack upon "the establishment." However I had experienced magnificent times of good attendance, great music, expanding programs of social concerns and evangelism. Now it was all coming to a close. Even though I was moving to another great church, I felt (on leaving Central) that I was abandoning a part of my life that I could never recover. With all of this crowding my mind and the experience at jurisdictional conference still playing over and over in my mind, I sat down to write the sermon. I entitled it: " On Losing and Leaving and Such Things".

There was a good attendance on July 27, 1980 in Central UMC, Fayetteville. The people came out of curiosity, love, loyalty to the church, to worship, and who knows for what other reasons. But they were there!. We had the usual good music and a stirring anthem, took up the offering (nothing must eliminate that), and now it was time for me to mount the pulpit, three steps above the chancel floor. I must be careful not to catch my toe in the hem of my robe, as I had done several times before. How many times had I tried to speak God's word from that pulpit? Fifty two (Sundays) times thirteen (years), minus vacations, plus funerals, minus times when the associate minister or visiting ministers were preaching … 600 times and more. I had told that congregation all I knew and a lot I didn't know. One more time I would ask the people to sit quietly and listen to me. As I think of it now, that is quite a request.

2

The Bargain

Penicillin was unknown. The sulpha drugs were just on the horizon. This was the reason my father died, unless, of course, a person can believe that God *wanted* my father to die in his early forties and at the peak of his effectiveness as a preacher. I do not believe that. God permitted his death, and in that sense it was his will, but to think that God *wanted* my father to die, leaving a wife, a baby son, a twelve-year-old son, and a college Freshman daughter, is to assign to God a disposition that would be despicable in a human being. So, if God did not want it to happen, and it did happen, does this mean that my father's death was beyond God's control? Yes and no! God has limited himself by his own laws—that is a "yes." Yet I have to remember that this limitation is a SELF-limitation—that is a "no." Does this line of reasoning mean that I am living in a "closed" universe of unrelenting cause and effect? No, I find no comfort in that. I believe in miracles, i.e., happenings that cannot be explained in naturalistic language. I believe that somewhere in this apparently closed circle of cause and effect there is an opening through which God moves to accomplish his purposes. This faith gives meaning to intercessory prayer. Why God intervenes sometimes and not at other times is beyond human understanding. I handle this problem by "faithing" it through. I faith; i.e., I act on the assumption that God is concerned for us whatever happens, and that He makes sense of events which appear to us as nonsense.

Moreover, this assumption that God acts for us is not simply choosing what is comfortable, as you might think from the previous paragraph. The reality of a realm independent of cause and effect, finds support not only in the well-known miracles, (e.g., the escape of the British Army at Dunkirk), but in a new science and mathematical development entitled "chaos." As I understand it, chaos describes those events which cannot be precisely predicted. These events have been observed in the orbits of solar bodies, in the pulsation of stars, in the mixing of fluids, in wave motion, oscillating chemical reactions, in electrical currents, in the dynamics of animal populations, even in heart beats. This chaos demonstrated in so many areas seems to infer that the universe is not sealed up like a biosphere but has an opening at the top, or somewhere, thru which a being like the God we know in Christ Jesus might enter.

Since, as a boy just turned twelve, I did not approach my father's death with theological "carry-on" baggage accumulated over eighty-seven years, I thought God might be amenable to a bargain. The bargain was simple: "God, you save my dad, and I'll become a minister of the gospel." Often I had heard the song "Rock of Ages," but my attempt to bargain with God showed that I didn't believe it, at least, I didn't believe that stanza which began, "In my hand no price I bring." Surely, I could do something, pay some price to influence God to save my father's life.

◆   ◆   ◆

He could not preach that Sunday morning, for the pain in his side was too intense. He had complained for a few days, but thought he would get better without a doctor. Now he lay flat on his back with his head propped up on two pillows. My mama sent for the doctor. He came quickly to the parsonage carrying his little black bag containing an assortment of pills and instruments, none of which would help my father. I did not know that then.

The doctor walked to my father's bedside, greeted him, shook down a thermometer that he had taken from an inside coat pocket, placed it under my father's tongue, reached for the pulse in my father's left wrist, snapped open a gold watch on a heavy chain, counting under his breath as the second hand moved around. He then asked where the pain was. My father laid his hand softly on his lower right side. The doctor pushed down gently on the indicated spot and released the pressure suddenly. Father grimaced in pain.

"He's got appendicitis." The doctor was calm and deliberate. Mama covered her face with her apron. Nestel, my sister, was away at college in Clarksville. Brother John was an infant. That was the immediate family.

I think we had guessed what was wrong with daddy, but we were not prepared for the doctor's next words.

"We must get him to the hospital quickly, for I fear the worst. His appendix may have ruptured."

We knew that was not good news, so we got busy with preparations for getting Dad to the hospital. We wasted no time. They took Dad to the hospital in Siloam Springs, ten miles from Gentry. It was a good hospital for that day and time. The surgery began promptly and in a little while the surgeon brought the feared news.

"His appendix has ruptured and peritonitis has set in," he said quietly. "We have inserted a tube to drain away the infection. We'll have to see what happens."

Over the next four days, I watched Father grow weaker and weaker. I prayed! How I prayed! Standing beside his bed that Thursday, my mind flashed back to the shop in which my father had taught me how to use basic hand tools—saw, hammer, square.

"Son, don't push down on the saw. Let it cut what it will. Make your strokes as long as the saw. Pull the saw backward to start your cut. Hold the hammer by the end of the handle. That way you'll get more power. Put the square's long end along the edge of the long side of the board."

The mental picture changed. I was in the squirrel woods with my father.

"The squirrel is on the other side of the tree, son. Go around the tree and shake a bush. That will make the squirrel come around to my side where I can shoot him."

"Come on, son, try to keep up." These were the repeated words of my father as we were hunting squirrels one day. I was a little tad and dad walked with the long strides of an Indian. Grandmother Cooper had said he was one-eighth Chickasaw, one of the five civilized tribes that settled in Oklahoma after the Trail of Tears. Dad *looked* Indian—black hair, high cheek bones, of a dark complexion, brown eyes. In the woods he *walked* like an Indian, quietly, carefully, and rapidly when the situation demanded it.

I had lost interest in the hunt, for the squirrels were not to be found that day. Moreover, my rubber boots were getting heavier by the minute. Suddenly my father raised his shotgun and fired at something on the ground in front of us.

"I think it was a bobcat," he said. "He jumped right out of that tree and hit the ground running."

From that time on during the hunt, his admonition to "keep up" changed radically.

"Stay off my heels," he said in exasperation, "you're pulling my boots off."

The woods fade away and suddenly I was sitting on a river bank with my father.

"Watch the cork. Wait until it goes under, then raise your pole quickly. Here, let me show you how to put a worm on the hook."

A groan came from the bed, and my thoughts came wobbling back to the unbearable tragedy playing out before my eyes. Father was dying. He had fought the spreading infection with all the strength he could muster, but it was not enough. The doctors said they had done all they could do. I had no reason to disagree, ignorant as I was about such matters, but is it not ironic that if this had taken place a few years later, my father would have lived? What today might be controlled easily by a modern drug was out of control in March of 1930.

Father's sermons and the teachings from Sunday School had convinced me that praying at such times was appropriate and effective. So I tried it. Praying was not new to me. Most of it had been the "now I lay me down to sleep" variety, or "God bless my mama and daddy, sister, brother, aunt, uncle, etc." This situation, however, called for a different kind of praying. I was desperate. All that persons could do for my father had been done. Prayer was all that was left. I prayed, and nothing happened as a result. How could I strengthen my case? Where the idea came from, I do not know, but I proposed to strike a bargain with God. Right there by the bedside of my dying father I laid out the bargain.

"Dear God, if you will save the life of my father, I will become a minister of the Gospel."

Now it is only fair to say that I had thought of being a minister before this moment, had preached a sermon in my father's church at Green Forrest when I was eleven; but it just seemed right, at this juncture, to promise God that I would really go through with it; i.e., if He would save my father's life. Dad died! Would it not have been great, if I could say that he <u>lived</u>? Not only would I have had my father for many years, I could have used the story to "prove" that God answers prayer. My struggle for faith across the years might not have been so fierce. Who knows? I don't remember thinking that God had not kept *His* side of the bargain. Perhaps I sensed that God had not agreed to my proposal. Nevertheless, my faith in God remained strong. Somehow, even *with* the death of my father, I knew I had to keep my side of the bargain.

3

"Faith of Our Fathers"

We had to move from Gentry. The church owned the parsonage, in accord with conference policy, and the next pastor would be coming soon to live where we had lived. No Methodist Church was without a pastor for long, because the bishop, on the advice of presiding elders, appointed pastors. These elders were ordained ministers who had been appointed by the bishop to supervise Methodist churches in certain geographical areas. At their best, they were pastors to the pastors. At their worst, they were little dictators. Our "sliding elder," as we called them behind their backs, was a pastor to *our* family at the time when we were desperately in need. He did what he could for us, but we knew we had to move.

Our roots were not in this town in western Arkansas on the Ozark plateau. We were from the "bottoms," that section of eastern Arkansas which was flooded now and then by the mighty Mississippi and her tributaries. The joke among preachers about the economic differences between the hill people and the "bottoms" people swirled around the saying, "In the hills, church members shout and pray, while in the bottoms, they cuss and pay."

Before we returned to the bottoms of the St. Francis River, we sojourned in the Ozark foothills in the town where my sister attended college. Mother wanted to give my sister, Nestel, the chance to finish her first year in the College of the Ozarks. The months spent from February to June in Clarksville are like a vague oblong blur in my mind. A boy's club offered boxing, wrestling, gymnastics, etc. That was it. I remember nothing about school, church, friends, although my sister insists that I should remember. What happened to those three months, and why are they blacked out? I can only guess that the death of my father was a blow so devastating that I was addled; i.e., unable to assimilate what was going on about me. So, I am not able to remember.

We moved in June to the town where Father had met Mother, where Sister and I had been born, Paragould, mother's hometown. Moving in with my mother's mother was not the best arrangement, but under the circumstances was the best mother could do. Three thousand dollars in insurance was not going to go far or last long. That was all the *money* that Father had left to us. However, our inheritance from him was rich.

My father believed in conversion. He believed in it, because it happened to him. Although he was not reared in a Christian home, he was attracted to the church. When he was nineteen years of age, he was "gloriously" converted in a revival meeting. For him this meant that God in Christ Jesus had not only forgiven his sins but had literally changed him, converted him, turned him around, made him into a different and better person. When my father talked about "being saved," he meant *converted*.

This change did not take place against his will. Like John Wesley, the English founder of the Methodist movement, he was an Armenian, a believer in free will. The part father played in the drama of salvation was the surrender of his will to God's will. God's part was the transforming of that will. Where one stopped and the other began, I find it difficult to say.

For my father, conversion happened instantaneously. I am sure he was not wholly ignorant of the Christian faith, but his parents had never trained him in it. He had never attended a church with any regularity. Somehow the power of the gospel took hold of him one night in a revival. He was moved to go down the aisle and fall on his knees at the mourner's bench. There he "prayed it thru," asking for God's saving grace to enter his life. It did! He arose from that bench knowing in his heart of hearts that God had saved him and that he had been converted. As far as I know, he never doubted that conversion experience.

I do not believe that father believed that his kind of experience of salvation was the only valid way a person could come to God, for he received me into the church on confession of faith when I was seven years of age. So he must have made room in his thinking for a variety of ways persons might experience the saving grace of God. But as long as he lived, he believed that a person, "sinking deep in sin far from the peaceful shore" could be lifted by the Master of the Sea.

Father also believed in a "heart felt" religion. When he was converted, he felt something. John Wesley, reporting on his experience in the prayer meeting on Aldersgate Street, London, said, "I felt my heart strangely warmed." My father had a similar experience. He felt release, acceptance, and joy. However, this felt faith was not a one time thing. Over and over across the years of his ministry, he felt God's presence in his life. He had a spiritual exuberance about him that was contagious.

During his first appointment in northeast Arkansas, he received an invitation to preach at a black Methodist Church. My mother said the black people enjoyed hearing him preach. It was not because he was a great theologian, not because of his oratory, nor because of his exquisite use of the King's English. These were not his characteristics, for his formal education ended at the eighth grade. Black Methodists loved to hear him preach because he preached with enthusiasm and sincerity. They believed that he believed what he was saying about Christian experience. The quote about him that I remember was attributed to some black Methodist. He said, "Reverend Cooper is the most religious *white* man I ever knew."

Father believed that if you had religion, you would *feel* it. He used to tell a story about one black minister talking with another about the spiritual condition of his flock. "Do your church members enjoy their religion?" The answer was quick and to the point: "Dem dat *has* it does." That was my father's belief. If a person has received the converting grace of God, he/she ought to feel it and enjoy it.

When I was about eight years old, my father was pastor of a small Methodist Church in a small town in northeast Arkansas, Marmaduke. He had invited a pastor friend to come and "help" him in a revival at the church. In those days the nightly meetings lasted two weeks at least. And it was during these special meetings, usually held in the summer after the crops had been laid by, that most people "got religion." This did not usually happen the first night of the meetings. People didn't get warmed up that quickly. Sometimes the meeting would be in the second week before sinners got under conviction. I remember that my father and the visiting minister, Bro.W.W. Peterson, were very distressed that no one had been converted in the first few days of the meeting. In the community there were some unconverted business men for whom my father had been praying. He had been praying that these men would be converted, but nothing had happened. This burdened my father. Then one night it happened. The meeting "broke," as they put it, and one of those men for whom father had been praying came down the aisle and gave his life to Christ. Others followed until a large number had come to the altar. There welled up within my father such a Christian joy that he was not able to control it. He began to shout for joy. You see, father was a 'shoutin' Methodist. He laughed and praised God. Even after the service when we had gone home, he continued to shout and laugh and praise God. I remember that in the divine confusion an old alarm clock was jarred from its place and clattered to the floor. Father just stood and looked at it and continued his praise of God who had wrought that night the miracle of conversion.

Father's religion was not all "sound and fury signifying nothing." He believed that Christian living meant *ethical* living. As far as he was concerned, the Bible laid down clear ethical standards, and the Christian was expected to live by these standards. He believed in the Ten Commandments and lived by them. For him the Golden Rule was a very useful measuring stick for behavior. I heard him talk about the DISCIPLINE of the Methodist Church, so I believe he was familiar with the General Rules given to Methodism by John Wesley; i.e., do all the good you can, avoid all the evil you can, and attend the ordinances of the church. Rules did not bother him. He did not think they restricted his freedom. He probably thought that they enhanced his freedom.

My father wanted to enhance my freedom, so he was not hesitant to impose rules upon me. At the time, I squirmed a bit under them; but, as I see them now, I realize that my father was teaching me something very important: there are right ways and wrong ways to behave. The right was good for me and pleasing to God, and the wrong was bad for everyone. Therefore, persons ought always to choose the good. Father reenforced this with a razor strap when I disobeyed, and reenforced it with love and companionship when I was a good boy—which, of course, was mooost of the time.

So I developed a conscience. There are many attitudes and actions which I cannot embrace to this day without feeling dirty and guilty. That situation does not mean that I have always refrained from doing what my conscience condemned. No, often I have refused to listen to the "still small voice," but God does not leave me alone. He leads me to repentance and extends to me his forgiveness. I am not as good a man as I ought to be, but I am better than I would have been, if I had not followed my father in believing that Christian living meant ethical living. Father did not leave us very much money, but he left us with concepts more precious than money.

Moving for a Methodist family is normal. In the early days of Methodism, pastors moved from one circuit to another almost every year. It has to be admitted that some preachers could not stay longer because they ran out of sermons. My father stayed longer than that in the charges he served. He stayed four years in each of three appointments or about that. Methodist preachers are assigned for one year at a time. As conference time approached, and moving became a possibility, clergy families were expected to clean house. My mother practiced this, and my wife, Bill, did too. The reason for the housecleaning was not so clear to me as a boy, but I soon learned that it was disgraceful for a pastor to move out of a parsonage without giving it a thorough cleaning. Not all ministers' wives felt as compulsive about this as mother did.

We did not have much to move from the Gentry parsonage, since the church furnished the furniture. I think we loaded it all into a pickup truck which my

Uncle Arthur Thief had driven to Gentry for my father's funeral. Heavily loaded, we set out across the state on mostly gravel roads to our destination on the eastern edge of Crowley's Ridge.

4

"When the Roll Is Called"

Grandmother Henley lived on the donic. I don't know the origin of the word "donic," nor even how to spell it. It was an area bounded on the east by the Eight Mile Creeks and on the west by the old creek bed which was left when the creek was straightened. My father and mother, when first married, had worked on the dredge boat which dug the new channel. It was to the donic that we moved in June of 1931.

The donic was not the elite section of Paragould, about as far from it as one could get. I think there were about ten houses on the donic. To say that these houses were modest is to exaggerate a bit, but families lived there. They had children, and children just naturally get together to play.

At the fiftieth reunion of my Paragould High School graduating class, Bill was visiting with someone who was one of my playmates from "donic" days. Bill said something about my "playing church" on the banks of the Eight Miles. The response from my playmate was quick and to the point: "He wasn't playing!"

I wasn't, I guess, although I was all of thirteen years of age. In any event, I gathered the donic kids together and led a church service. It was mostly singing. One favorite was: "When the Role is Called Up Yonder." We soon learned to belt it out with vigor, if not always on key. I know, dear reader, that this is hard to believe given the entertainment which modern young people demand, but it did happen. Moreover, good things came of it.

The donic children, following the example of their parents, no doubt, were not always careful in their use of expletives. To put it more succinctly—they could swear like sailors. In some of my "sermons" preached on the banks of the Eight Mile Creek, I pointed out that swearing was "taking the Lord's name in vain" and that this was specifically forbidden in the Ten Commandments found in the Bible. Nevertheless, bad habits are hard to break, and my donic friends would forget from time to time, if sufficiently provoked, and let loose a string of cuss words. However, more than once a quick prayer would follow the cuss words," "O Lord, forgive me."

The "religion" about which we sang and talked was "other worldly"; i.e., it dealt with what lay in store for us when we die. It was clear to me, then, that this was either heaven or hell, and I never doubted the beauty of one nor the temperature of the other. I don't remember thinking much about the love of God. God was an impartial judge who would see to it that we got what we deserved. Obviously, this put a heavy responsibility upon all of us, but I do not remember thinking that it was unbearably heavy. It was a simplistic ethic that made this acceptance of salvation by works easy. Being a "good" boy was not all that hard. It had nothing to do with race relations, sexual preference, social, political, and economic justice, war and peace, drugs, capital punishment, abortion, etc., all the issues which complicate our lives today and make salvation impossible if achieved by works. Being good was: avoiding cursing and foul language, not using alcohol, not having sex, obeying our parents, acknowledging God, praying, reading the Bible, going to church, washing our "neck 'n ears"—pious things.

Of course, I have long since abandoned this inadequate definition of goodness, but whether I have abandoned my efforts to save myself is open to question. Looking back across these years, I realize that much of the time I was living on the assumption that if I could do enough good, I would have it made.

The dividing line between "playing church" and "real church" is fuzzy in my mind. I can hardly tell when one stopped and the other began, for soon after those donic days they gave me a Local Preacher's License in the Methodist Episcopal Church, South. It was during the Paragould District Conference. The Reverend Doctor E.T. Wayland, was the Presiding Elder. That memorable date is October 15, 1932. I was fourteen years of age.

Robert N. Arbaugh, almost lifelong friend, was licensed to preach at this same District Conference. Robert lived just across the street from me, was three years older, preceding me to Hendrix College and Duke School of Religion, later named Duke Divinity School. Robert went to Missouri to do his ministry, but we have kept in touch all across the years.

Milk and butter were basic foods during the Great Depression. To make sure our family had these basics, mother bought a milk cow, Ole Bossie. We did not live in the open country where pastures would be available, but the back of our lot joined the drying yard of a barrel factory where there was plenty of free grazing room. Prohibition was the law of the land in those days, so the whiskey industry was not ordering many barrels. That meant that there were not many staves stacked in the yard, leaving acres and acres of green grass on which several cows could be found grazing happily, including Bossie.

There were no fences around the drying yard, so we tethered the cows on long chains. Bossie was my responsibility and my undoing, almost. Early every morning, I would go to the cow shed, milk the cow, lead her out into the drying yard, find a good grazing spot, and drive the stake to which I tied her with a long chain. At noon I went back to Ole Bossie, pulled up the stake, led her to the watering trough, and then led her back to another spot in the yard. In the evenings I went back for Ole Bossie, pulled the stake, took her to the watering trough, led her back to the cow shed, milked and fed her. This happened day after day, same routine. Moreover, Ole Bossie was a rouge cow, breaking into gardens, if she had the least opportunity. She was a pain to milk, hitting me in the face with a tail full of cockleburs, stepping into the pail of milk, throwing her head at the flies. It was all so exasperating that I threatened mother one day, "Mother, if you do not sell that cow, I am sure I cannot go into the ministry." I forget the timing, but she sold the cow.

Francis Bland, my high school and college classmate and friend from these years, likes to tell about my first day in Paragould High School. He was sitting just behind me in eight grade math. Mrs. Thacker, a hard-nosed teacher but wanting to get acquainted, walked up behind me and playfully pulled my hair. As I recall, I had done nothing wrong, but my heart was still tender from the wounds of losing my father, so I burst into tears. This embarrassed Mrs. Thacker. She turned to Francis, hit him solidly in the stomach and said, "We're always joking around, aren't we Francis?"

It was "the worst of years," the thirties, the Great Depression. The stock market had tumbled and the economy had slowed to less than a snail's pace. Unemployment was very high. Millions in this country did not have enough to eat. The government had a program to give basic food, called commodities, to those who needed it. Flour, cooking oils, beans, corn meal, canned goods were some commodities. People would form long lines when the commodities were being distributed. It was a difficult time for many families, including ours.

My mother got a government job teaching people how to can vegetables, fruits, and meats. She also made visits in homes checking on the needs of people and teaching them cooking skills, etc. She could not drive, so I drove her (age 12-14) in our model A Ford. It was my first time to see abject poverty. Some homes we visited were incredible—dirt floors, little furniture, ragged clothing, inadequate heating and no cooling, no window screens, very little to cook with and nothing to cook, and no basic health or housekeeping skills. Mercy!

On every freight train that came thru Paragould, one could see hoboes, as they were called. Many men were simply looking for a job, moving from place to place. They would get off the train and start down Lake Street, knocking on doors, and asking for food, e.g., "Could you spare a little coffee?" Sometimes they would ask for sugar or a potato. Often they would take the food to a camp near an abandoned stave mill, cook it, and share it with others. We were afraid of these people.

My mother never tried to scare me into goodness by mentioning the devil, but all the kids on the donic knew about Paragould Slim. He was a mythical character, inspired by the hoboes (I think). He carried a sack on his back containing "who knows what." I think I remember being told, "If you do that, Paragould Slim will get you." But I viewed this character much like I viewed Santa Claus on the other end of the spectrum, i.e., with some doubt but with practical respect.

Living was not easy for us. I remember that my mother traded my deceased father's 12 gauge shot gun for credit on a grocery bill. Later I tried to trace down this shotgun, thinking I would buy it back, but it had passed thru too many hands. Some owners had died. The gun was lost. However, I did manage to buy a 410-gauge shotgun single shot. I sold it to my uncle, Arthur Thiel, and bought a 22 single shot rifle. The ammunition was cheaper.

I shined shoes in a barber shop for five cents a pair. You could get a hair cut for twenty-five cents, a hamburger for a dime and a coke or Dr. Pepper for five cents. We hunted and ate rabbits, called Hoover Hounds, after Herbert Hoover, our president in the early days of the depression. Eldridge Goodman and I tried to trap rabbits, but someone beat us to our traps every morning. We knew we were catching rabbits, fur was everywhere, but we never had a rabbit in the trap. One morning we got up real early and caught the man running our trap. We shot in the air to scare him away. He yelled that he would whip us, if we would throw down our gun. We didn't and he didn't. I still remember his name. There is a prominent United Methodist Minister with the same name, but, no, it couldn't be....

One year the public schools could not stay open. There was not enough money from taxes. The school board decided that they would charge tuition. My tuition was $4.00 a month. I made $1.25 cents a week carrying papers. If I sold ten extra papers in a week, I would get three cents each for them, so most of the time I made thirty cents more. Out of this I saved $1.00 of each week's pay to take care of my tuition in school. I brought the dollar home each week and put it in a glass in the cabinet. I could spend the rest of my money as I wanted. It usually went for cokes, ice cream, but sometimes when we were going camping, I would buy a pack of Chesterfields. However, I did not "take up" smoking, not until seminary days, at least.

My speech teacher was Mrs. Pearce who taught that subject in high school, was the dramatic coach, etc. I had parts in several plays, entered oration contests (won some)—all under Mrs. Marie Thost Pearce. One day she offered to give me private speech lessons. When I told her that I could not afford it, she asked if my mother would be willing to do her washing. Mother agreed to this and each week as I took my speech lessons, I would carry the clean clothes in and the dirty ones out.

Somehow, I saved up enough money to buy a tennis racket. It would cost about $5.00. Mother didn't want me to spend the five dollars that way. I really needed it to buy clothes. But tennis was more important than clothes at that time in my life. We played with the balls until they didn't have any felt left on them and would hardly bounce. We just couldn't afford to buy new ones very often, and if you sliced them just right, they were impossible to return. We called them drop shots.

It cost a dime to go to the movies. Sometimes I didn't have a dime, but the popcorn aroma blowing out of the theater and the billboards advertizing the latest adventures of Ken Maynard or Tom Mix were more than I could resist. So I would hurry to the junk yard to pick up some iron to sell. Copper brought more than iron.

I don't remember worrying too much about the depression, although I know mother did. Nearly everybody was in the same boat. Our pleasures were simple, but we had a good time anyway.

Most people did not know that smoking was so dangerous to your health. But store-bought cigarettes were high, although only fifteen cents a pack. Many people rolled their own cigarettes to save money. "Golden Grain" was a favorite tobacco. It came in a little sack about as big as a cigarette pack. "Rolling your own" was quite an art. You held the paper in your left hand, the paper cupped to hold the tobacco. Then, with your right hand, you would sprinkle the tobacco into the paper. Then you tightened the string on the tobacco pouch with your teeth and put it in your pocket. Then you would carefully roll the paper around the tobacco, licking the edge of the paper to make it stick, and not forgetting to twist the end to keep the tobacco from falling out.

Some people had little mechanical cigarette rollers. I believe they used a brand of tobacco called "Bugle." The tobacco was of a different cut than "Golden Grain." "Prince Albert" was another brand of tobacco. A favorite prank was to call up a store and ask, "Do you have Prince Albert in a can? " When the clerk would answer, "Yes," we would say, "Well, you had better let him out or he will smother." Bad.

We always had enough food to eat. Mother was a good manager. My sister worked at the "dime store," Sterlings, I think. Her pay was meager, but it helped a lot.

We lived in a house which mother had bought with some of my dad's insurance money. I think it cost $1200-$1500. We always called it the "ole shoe," because of its strange shape. We made it into a duplex when my sister, Nestel, got married to Dick Woodward. They had one child, Sue Carolyn.

When Roosevelt became president, the government developed work projects, WPA and others. People called the WPA projects "we piddle along" projects, because some workers didn't seem to work very hard, leaning on their shovels, etc.

It was a difficult time in this country. A revolution might have developed, but no one came along to lead it. However, I think some were standing in the wings. In Germany, there was Hitler.

Now that I had a License to Preach, I was invited to preach in the rural churches around Paragould. Usually, the church people would give me a little money. It helped financially, and it gave me practice in preaching. Mostly, it was a case of poor pay for poor preaching.

One day the Presiding Elder, A. W. Martin, told me that the pastor of Cache Lake Church had resigned, and that he wanted me to go up there (nineteen miles north of Paragould) and be the pastor. So I began my first pastorate. The church was organized. It had a membership roll and met in a school house. I would go up Sunday morning, preach, eat dinner with someone, and preach again that night. It was an exhilarating experience for a boy still in high school but kept me humping to get enough sermons ready.

Cache Lake Methodist Church met in a school house near an "s" curve on old Highway One. It was a one room, frame structure about twenty feet long and fifteen feet wide. It was equipped with school desks. For church services, we would stretch planks across the seats of the desks, making room for more people. It was lighted with gasoline lanterns which some members brought from their homes. I don't think we had a piano, but I am not sure.

Someone asked me if I could marry a couple. I believe I must have asked my presiding elder about this. After telling me I must have my Local Preacher's License recorded in the Court House, he said it would be all right. I was fourteen or fifteen years of age when I married my first couple. I do not remember the names, but many years later the couple identified themselves after I had preached at Prewitt's Chapel, Paragould. My Local Preacher's License is recorded in Greene County, Arkansas, Book A, page 273. (In later years, I went to the Greene County court house and asked to see Book A. They told me that it had been lost, but Francis Bland told me that he thinks it was moved to another place for storage.)

The members of the Cache Lake Church were farmers. The land was good and some made a fair living; but, cash was not plentiful, even though their community was called "Cache Lake". Sorry about that. I stayed in several of their homes during my tenure as pastor there. Later some of these people died of tuberculosis. I was grateful that I did not get infected.

Summer revivals continued to be the doors thru which most people entered the church. They were almost obligatory. So, revival time came. The presiding elder, A. W. Martin, said that we would take "time-about" preaching. That was great, because I didn't have enough sermons for a week of preaching. All went well, until pressing business called the P.E. to some other part of the state, leaving me alone to continue the "meeting", the word often used for revivals. I preached that first night, gave the invitation, and nothing happened. No one came forward to give their lives to Jesus. I was brokenhearted. When I talked with my mother about this, she said, "There are a lot of things you have to leave up to the Lord." The next night I preached again and gave the invitation. Someone came forward, then others, finally nineteen. The people were so happy! They just milled around and hugged each other and shouted for joy. I felt like I was on top of the world. I never had an experience exactly like that again.

My mother's advice during the revival to leave some things to God, was something she practiced. My father's death rocked her back on her heels, but she was able somehow to regain her balance. I think it was her faith in God that "saw her thru" those dreary days. She was left a widow in the Great Depression with three children, one in college, one just out of diapers, and one teenager, yours truly. I don't know how she managed to give us what we needed, but she did. She trusted in God to help her, (and, He did, I am sure) but she worked as if everything depended upon her management.

That mother was a good money manager, everyone in the family agreed. Tight? Maybe, but she had to be. If I just had to have a nickel for something, I could go to her. She would scratch around in a drawer or somewhere and pull out a little handkerchief in which she had tied up some coins. This she would untie and produce the necessary nickel, or dime, if circumstances warranted.

Her formal education was scanty. She told me that her mother, who had a house full of younger kids, wanted her to stay home from school to help with the family. Consequently, mother was not able to go beyond the sixth grade in school.

Mother's formal education was just a beginning. She became an educated person by reading, and was an active leader in women's work in the church. In her fifties she was the teacher of an Adult Class in Griffin Memorial Methodist Church, Paragould. As I visited home during my college and seminary days, I would talk with her about theology. She often surprised me with the liberal point of view she expressed. Biblical criticism did not bother her.

The making of pastoral appointments in the conference was always of great interest to mother. She prided herself on her ability to do "kitchen cabinet"work, i.e., to predict what preacher would be appointed to which charge. I do not remember that she ever criticized her pastor, whoever it might be. I can imagine that she did, but it must have been an "exception to the rule," or I would have remembered. Having been the wife of a minister, she knew the problems some ministers face and was generous in her support of her pastor.

Mother was an exceptionally good cook. My wife, Bill, has heard this often enough, I am sure, but it was the truth. Mother cooked for the crew of the dredge boat that dug the "Eight Mile"drainage ditch. Later this ditch was renamed "The Francis Bland Floodway," in honor of my friend who had worked so hard for so many years to get the governmental funding for the project.

It was fortunate for all of us that mother married Ben F. McAden, a widower who was a member of Griffin Memorial Methodist Church. (Incidentally, they named the church for Ben McAden's relative, Rev. H.H. Griffin, who had been pastor of the church which they called East Side Methodist in its beginning days.) Daddy Mac, as we called him, worked at the Post Office as a custodian. The job paid very well, by our standards, and insured that mother would be "taken care of." Nestel had married; I was a senior in high school, planning to go to Hendrix College; my brother, John, was just starting in the first grade. Things were looking up.

Ben McAden was of the old school. He sang by "shaped" notes. He could pick up a song book, and start a song in the right key and pitch just by looking at the shape of the notes. He died after about twenty years of marriage to my mother. They were mostly good years. Mother continued to live happily until she died in 1985, although the last few years of her life were spent in Greene Acres Nursing Home, Paragould. Arthritis had crippled her so severely that home care was not practical.

We planned a little party at the nursing home for mother on her ninetieth birthday. We rolled her out of her room in a wheel chair and placed her at the head of a table in the dining room. We had a good meal, brought out the cake with several candles (not ninety). As I recall, mother was not able to cut the cake. Her knurled and twisted fingers made that impossible. However, I think she blew out some candles. Then she surprised us by saying, "I know a song I would like to sing." Of course, we encouraged her. As a young woman, she had a nice singing voice, but now it crackled and popped. Nevertheless, it was music to our ears to hear her sing "What a friend "I". (she changed the wording to the first person, making it a very personal thing)—"What a Friend I have in Jesus, all my sins and griefs to bear, what a privilege to carry everything to God in prayer. O what peace I often forfeit, oh, what needless pain I bear, all because I do not carry everything to God in prayer." I don't think there was a dry eye around the table, but mother was not thru. She said, "I know another stanza." We laughed and she sang the second stanza without missing a word.

My brother, John, and I were standing at her bedside when she breathed her last. Together we prayed, "Our Father, who art in heaven."

The new "converts" from the meeting in the Cache Lake school house would need to be baptized. The Black River, being not many miles away, was chosen as the place for this special service. When the selected Sunday afternoon arrived, the congregation met on the banks of the river near Knobel, Arkansas. Another denominational congregation had arrived about the same time the Methodists reached the river. They started a service. We listened. Soon the preacher of this other denomination felt it was his duty to point out the inadequacies of the Methodist Church and this young preacher in particular. I don't remember being disturbed, but my people were.

Nevertheless, I baptized my converts. You must understand that I had never baptized anyone before and had only a witness' knowledge of how it should be done. I had seen my father and other ministers do it, so I was undaunted. I led the candidates (as they were called) out into the water, being careful not to lead them into a deep hole. Actually, someone had already stuck a stick out in the water to indicate the safety zone. I brought the first convert around, asked them to hold my right wrist with both hands. Then, putting my left arm behind their backs, I laid them over in the water, completely submerging them. Now, what I learned was: don't baptize people down stream. The water runs up their noses, if they don't hold them, and it is difficult to pull them back up with the current of the water pushing them down. Another thing I learned: it is difficult to baptize a fat person. They tend to float like a cork, and sometimes it takes an extra effort to get them completely "under'. In good time it was all accomplished.

I was not a "jock"; i.e., I did not play football or basketball for Paragould High. However, I did play "pickup" baseball and "shinny". This game was similar to hockey; i.e., the object of the game was to hit the puck over the opponent's goal line. We made our sticks out of a sapling which we pulled from the ground root and all. We shaped the crook from the root. The puck was a tin can. Pet Milk cans made the best pucks. But after they had been hit a few hundred times, they became dangerous metal missiles which caused many a cut or bruise on the players. You can guess why this game was called "shinny". I took many wacks on my shins, sometimes administered by accident and sometimes otherwise. It was supposed to strike fear to the hearts of our opponents when we yelled, "shin-neeeeeey".

Shinny was the game we played while waiting for the papers to come off the press in the afternoons after school. Besides the money earned, carrying papers was a good experience for a growing boy. It developed leg muscles and lungs. They did not allow us to ride bicycles. We walked—with our papers in a home-made cloth sack slung over the shoulder and hanging down in front to be handy for folding the papers. The *Daily Press* was not a big paper, usually consisting of six pages, so I folded it into a neat little package just right for sailing onto the porches of our subscribers. I got quite good at sailing the papers, although sometimes a paper would sail up on a roof. That was bad, for we had to account for every paper and a mis-thrown paper was not an acceptable excuse for a shortage.

About lung capacity: Just as we left the "Daily Press" office, Miss Irma would say, "Cry your papers." We did most of the time, choosing a headline we thought might entice someone to buy an "extra" paper. For twenty-five cents a person could subscribe to the paper for two weeks, payment in advance. A single copy of the paper cost five cents. If I sold as many as ten "extras" in a week, they would pay me three cents each. Many a week I did not sell as many as ten. When that happened, they paid me two cents a copy. It didn't take us long to figure out a scheme. If we came to the end of the week with nine papers sold, we would dig down for a nickel and buy a paper for ourselves to bring our total to ten. That way we would get thirty cents instead of eighteen. Of course, if you subtract the five cents we paid, the net would be only seven cents. But a penny was a penny in those days. I could buy a stick of gum with a penny, or a jawbreaker (round hard candy).

Eldridge Goodman, a very good friend who worked at the "Daily Press" before I did, was responsible for getting me the job carrying papers. When an opening came for a carrier, he ran all the way across town to get me. Near the end of his life, he reminded me of this. A few months later I "had his funeral", an expression we used to say that we had conducted the funeral of someone. Eldridge was an inseparable friend during my junior and senior high school days. We hunted together, played together, and were just together, hanging out, I think is the current word for this. For economic reasons he did not go to college, but that does not mean that he was uneducated. I have never known anyone who pursued knowledge as he did. He took correspondence courses, night courses, and read extensively.

Eldridge did not profess the Christian faith until he was about forty years of age. We talked about it many times in those years of our adolescence, but he did not join a church. His parents were Baptists, but he was always a bit more liberal than most Baptists in those days. However, he did join the Baptist Church late in life. I encouraged him to do it, because his second wife was a strong Baptist. But I am getting ahead of my story. Sometime in the 1950's, he called me from Memphis and said that he was to be confirmed in the Episcopal Church and that I must come. I explained to him that I had to preach on Sundays. (I was pastor of First Church Conway at the time.) He would not take "no" for an answer. He said something to this effect: "You tried hard enough to get me into the church when we were boys together. Now that I have decided to do it, you are going to be here." And I was—traveling to Memphis in a bus because the roads were under a heavy snow. After I retired, his wife called me saying, "Eldridge died last night. Will you come to Monroe and give the message at his funeral?" I did.

The five years in Paragould High School were very formative. I am especially indebted to Miss Ruth Weber and Mrs. Viola Stone, teachers, and to Mr. Clifford Blackburn, school superintendent. They gave me the basics and supplemented that with opportunities and encouragement. Opal Houston Starr was a pretty and young teacher who tried to teach me Latin. I did learn, "amo, amos, amont" and "omnia Gallia est tres parte." I had a crush on Miss Star.

For the record, I was not the best student, not all "A's", not a valedictorian. I made the honor roll several times, as I recall, but I was not a "brain". I was involved in activities of all kinds, except, as I have said, athletics. Drama, declamation, school politics—these were very important to me. I was a Thespian, a member of a dramatic society. I was a member of the National Honor Society, and during my senior year, I was elected President of the Student Body.

I lived on the East side in Paragould, i.e., east of the railroad tracks. Whether the "Westsiders" considered the "Eastsiders" second class or not, I will not say, but some of us from the East side felt that they did. It was always a source of satisfaction when someone from the East Side excelled in something. The Ketchum boys, Hugh and Percy, were good football players. Elmer Downs was an all-around athlete and an almost perfect physical specimen. East Side wasn't doing badly!

The years in Paragould High School were times for growing up. There were girls, of course, to whom I gave increasing attention as my hormones kicked in. The first one I was "serious"about was a year or two older, and may have been the one who introduced me to kissing. Understand that this kissing was not what you see on television today; i.e., one person attempting to swallow another. Kissing was "as far as we went." In this connection, there were parties where we played spin the bottle. Boys and girls would sit in a circle. Someone, out in the middle of the circle, would spin a milk bottle. The person to whom the bottle pointed was the person with whom the spinner would walk around the block. Or, I believe, a kiss could be given instead of the walk. I remember that I approached this game with some trepidation, not wanting to walk with or be kissed by just anyone. I do not take credit for remaining a virgin thru these years. As far as I knew, nice young people were not sexually active in high school. Occasionally, we would hear that some girl was an easy make, and that some fellow had gotten "in her pants," but this was far from being the rule. So it was the times, my religious convictions, and the normal fears which enabled me to reach marriage without having "gone to bed" with anyone.

I graduated from Paragould High School in 1936, one hundred years after the Battle of the Alamo, the beginning of Arkansas statehood, and the organization of the Arkansas Conference of the Methodist Episcopal Church in Batesville, Arkansas.

From the time I decided to be a minister of the gospel, I planned to attend Hendrix College, the Methodist college in Arkansas. But before I embarked on that pilgrimage with Francis Bland, who was to be my room mate for four years, I had an experience which changed my life forever, about which I now have some regrets. Moreover, a little maturity somehow made less palatable the creek bank song, "When the Roll is Called Up Yonder". I was beginning to see that Christian living was not as simple as I thought. And with the ethical complexity came the discomforting thought that I just may not be able to work out my own salvation. About then, the words of that old hymn scrolled across the bottom of the screen of my mind, "In my hand no price I bring. Simply to the cross I cling."

5

To Kill or Not to Kill

I had known since early childhood that there was a commandment which read, "Thou shalt not kill," but I never dreamed that this might be applied to our national enemies. War between nations was something I accepted as a matter of course and of considerable interest. I remember being drawn to pictures of World War I weapons, the Colt 45 automatic, the machine guns (Maxim, I think), the Springfield rifles. My folks thought I was being studious when I dragged down the old "World Books", but I was just drooling over the pictures of guns.

I have already referred to my father's gun and to the guns I owned, but ownership was not enough. We hunted with the guns. Eldridge Goodman, Howard Hollis and I would spotlight rabbits with a carbide lamp (like early coal miners used). It was a favorite sport. Someone told us that in spotlighting you will see only one eye of the rabbit, a dull red. That always seemed amusing, for everybody knew rabbits have two eyes. However, on closer examination of the dead rabbits, we noticed that the eyes were on the sides of the head. It is no wonder we spotted only one eye of the rabbit.

We did our spotlighting while walking along the old P S & E railroad track. Trains were infrequent, so we walked along in comparative safety, shining our lights out into the brush. When we saw the red dot, we would aim our guns at the dot and let go a round. We didn't miss often, because we were fairly close to the quarry and because we used shot guns.

We were careful about cleaning the rabbits, for we had heard about rabbit fever, and wanted no part of that. Also, in the skinning process, we looked for what we called "wolves," lumps in the rabbit's fur, caused, I think, by parasites. If the lumps were found, we did not eat the rabbit.

Squirrel hunting was also a favorite sport. A successful hunt usually meant that we got up and out to the woods just as day was breaking, the time when squirrels are most active. Slipping thru the woods, we would see a squirrel and shoot it, if we could, which wasn't always. One morning, as I sat on a log watching a tree in which I had seen a den hole, a squirrel came out of the hole, down the tree to the ground, straight toward me. All the time, I was trying to get the gun on him. Would you believe that this squirrel ran right between my legs, and I haven't fired my gun yet?

We formed a club, three or four of us. All went well, until one member brought a pistol to our club house. We thought this was too dangerous, maybe illegal, and asked that member not to bring the pistol again. I don't know whether there is any connection or not, but the last time I saw this person he was in jail.

I relate these things in this chapter to contrast my interest in guns with what was to happen to me, and, of course, because I wanted to get these things into the story somewhere.

It was 1935 that the Methodist Church planned a National Youth Conference to be held in Memphis, Tennessee during the Christmas break from school. I was in the eleventh grade, and wanted to attend this conference, but money was the problem. Somehow, Miss Ruth Webber, one of my teachers, learned of my predicament and gave me the money to attend the conference. Little did I know, when I started to Memphis, that this conference would change my life significantly.

The sermons and lectures which I heard at this conference introduced me to pacifism, a doctrine which tries to take literally the commandment, "Thou shalt not kill." It was clear that many of the speakers meant, "Thou shalt not kill, even if your country is invaded, even if your own life is in jeopardy." I bought this doctrine, "lock, stock, and barrel." (I realize this expression in this context mixes things up a bit.)

Also, I was introduced to the hymn "Are Ye Able?" What a thrilling experience it was to hear a thousand young people singing,

"Are ye able, said the Master,
"To be crucified with me?"

We knew that those who held firmly to pacifism would pay a price. It would not be a popular position, we were told. Persecution would be inevitable. But many of us were all but hypnotized by the exhilarating challenge to take seriously Jesus' statement about "turning cheeks".

On returning home to my church in Paragould, I became an advocate for pacifism, speaking here and there to youth groups.

During my four years at Hendrix (1936-1940), I did not waver in my devotion to this doctrine of non-violence. A good number of students took the same position, and we did what we could to counter the war spirit that was beginning to emerge on campus.

The draft came into effect, and I registered as a conscientious objector. As a ministerial student, I was automatically classified " 4-D". After entering seminary at Duke School of Religion (the school's name at that time), I became convinced that it was not right for me to accept "4-D" classification when I was a pacifist. So I asked the Draft Board in Greene County, Arkansas, to grant me the classification "4-E" as a conscientious objector. They denied this request, thinking, I am sure, that I must be stupid or something, not accepting "4-D". I then appealed my request, but before any resolution of this matter, I decided I would just accept the "4-D" classification, and wrote the Draft Board to that effect. (I still have a copy of this letter.) I was beginning to doubt my pacifist position, and considered (I am not sure how seriously) entering the armed services as a chaplain.

As Byron Cravens, my seminary room mate, and I rode the trains between Durham, North Carolina and Arkansas, I would tell soldiers that I was finishing seminary and would ask them, "Should I join the chaplaincy or go back home and take a church?" I do not remember that a single soldier ever told me to join the chaplaincy. They said, "Go home and take care of the people there." That is what I did, eventually.

As I look back across the pages of my life, one of my regrets is that I did not join the chaplaincy to help my country defeat Hitler. Looking for an excuse, I might point to my ignorance of the extent of the wickedness of the Nazi regime. I know now that Hitler had to be stopped, that turning the other cheek would not work. I should have had a part in stopping him. It may be that I feel guilty for having lived thru the war while so many died.

This does not mean that I have changed from a pacifist to a warmonger. No, it means that I have come to believe that I simply cannot be a pacifist under every circumstance, and that there are some evils so tremendous that they must be resisted with force. I cannot say that Jesus would ever be violent, or that he would approve of violence, but I know that there are some circumstances under which I would be violent. All I can do then is to ask for God's forgiveness. "War is hell," Sherman said. And it is, but there are some conditions worse. Nevertheless, there is no such thing as a "holy" war, not even if we wage it against those who make such claims for their actions. Force cannot solve the problems of the world, but, at times, it can open an opportunity for a solution of the problems.

I believe that our nation should lead in making peace between the warring factions on this planet. I believe we are doing this, to some extent, but I could hope we might double and redouble our efforts. We must broker a peace in the middle east, in Asia, in Africa, in Iraq, and Afghanistan. To do this, we must have adequate conventional forces and state of the art military equipment. This country's obvious leadership among the nations of the world obligates it to make what contributions it can to peace.

I print a sermon here because it represents my present thinking on the subject of this chapter.

"It was sixty three years and four wars ago that I attended the National Youth Conference in Memphis. That is where I first saw the glory of disarmament and peace. During this conference I began to see that God did not want nations fighting with each other, and that I ought to be doing whatever I could to keep it from happening. In my mind's eye, for the first time, I saw a world disarmed and at peace.

The exile prophet, Micah, had seen that glory long centuries before I saw it. I do not know what part of Judah he came from, but he had experience with wars. His little nation lay in the natural path of the great powers from the north and south as they fought with each other. As a result, his nation was constantly under the gun, so to speak. Finally the armies of Nebuchadnezzar overran Judah and carried captive her leaders, including our poet-prophet. So his idealistic dreams of peace did not spring from an international naivete. He knew about the grim realities of international intrigue, but his faith eyes had seen the glory of peace. Hear his beautiful and moving words: "They shall beat their swords into plowshares and their spears into pruning hooks; nations shall not lift up sword against nation, neither shall they learn war anymore."

I saw that glory, too, four wars ago, as I have said. But, as CNN shows every minute, the nations have not fashioned their instruments of destruction into tools of production, and they have not stopped learning how to wage war. We learn more and more about it every day, but I'll never forget the glory I saw during those December days of 1935. That dream of disarmament and peace still haunts me. I welcome every move made toward mutual disarmament and a just peace, and I cannot, will not, accept war as the inevitable nature of the future. War has come; but, beyond the smoke of battle, my eyes of faith can see peace, enduring peace.

Perhaps I can underline this point by a reference to Tennyson's "Locksley Hall," written more than a century ago. The character in the poem, presumably Tennyson himself, had returned from a nostalgic visit to old haunts. After he had reminisced about the past, he turned his thoughts to the future and described the glory of a world at peace. True, he saw it thru the smoke of battle, remarkably modern. But Tennyson saw the glory of peace. Hear it:

> "Far along the worldwide whisper
> Of the south wind rushing warm,
> With the standards of the people
> Plunging thru the thunderstorm;
> Till the war drums throbbed no longer,
> And the battle flags were furl'd
> In the Parliament of Man,
> The Federation of the world".

If you ask me how far it is to disarmament and peace, I have to say I don't know how far. It could be a long ways, but it could be just around the corner too. I hope and pray that the "new world order", about which President Bush talked, will become a reality. Whatever the situation, I am convinced that in our mind's eye we must continue to see the glory of disarmament and peace, if we are to have a chance of achieving it. I don't argue for unilateral disarmament. That might invite war. I said mutual disarmament, just peace. What I am saying is that we must never forget the direction we are to travel, the ultimate goal—peace, permanent peace. And we must never cease working to achieve it and never rely ultimately on might and megatonage. Peace! Mine eyes have seen it. It is a dream that draws me! Do you see it? Hear the Kipling words:

> "For heathen heart that puts her trust
> In reeking tube and iron shard;
> All valiant dust that builds on dust,
> And guarding calls not Thee to guard.
> Lord God of hosts, be with us yet,
> Lest we forget, lest we forget."

If this sounds like preaching, "not to worry, mate". It IS preaching! Could you expect anything else from a preacher?

6

Bleeding Heart

I cannot remember when I first decided I would go to Hendrix College after high school. It was just something accepted at our house. Mother and I didn't know how we could afford it. Nevertheless, I was going, and that was that. Hendrix was a Methodist College, and in those days was the primary school for Arkansas Methodist ministerial students, enrolling as many as one hundred at some point between 1936 and 1940.

The green of our Freshman caps was truly symbolic of those of us entering Hendrix College in 1936. Francis Bland and I were among these, hopefully not the greenest of the green. We arrived on campus a bit fearful of the upper class-men who helped us learn very soon that we were second class citizens of the school. It was "Freshman, do this" or "Freshman, strike a brace." We obeyed when cornered, but soon learned ways of avoiding a confrontation.

Francis Bland played such an important role in my life at Hendrix, and his name appears so often in these writings, that I must say several things about him. We were room mates for four years, so I know what I am talking about. When he came to Hendrix he was shy–I mean girl shy. I am sure that he didn't have more than one or two dates in our four years at Hendrix. He didn't need to be shy for he was a very capable, interesting, affable person, a "good catch".

Surely Francis and I had some disagreements, living in the close quarters of a college dorm, but for the life of me I cannot remember one now. Since his family owned the Dr. Pepper plant in Paragould, we always had Dr. Peppers in our room. But it was before the days of small refrigerators, so to have a cold Doc we had to go down to the ground floor to the water cooler in which there was always a chunk of ice. Chips of this ice did the trick.

Since Francis and I came from the same hometown, his family often let me ride with them when they came to pick up Francis. I was blessed to have him as a room mate.

After graduation and until after the war, Francis worked in a defense plant in Memphis. Returning home to Paragould, he began working in the family-owned Dr. Pepper Bottling plant. At some point in these days, he met Winnie. He must have been so "smitten" that he threw caution to the wind, dating and marrying her. Then he began a long life of extraordinary service to family, church, community, and his business. He excelled in each of these areas. His shyness disappeared; his personality reversed itself. He became a very confident and outgoing business leader who was to be found on the right side of every church and community endeavor. His interest in athletics brought him recognition upon recognition. Every good movement in Paragould had his support. Often, before they undertook a venture, he was consulted and his support and leadership solicited. He developed into one of the most respected, influential, and admired men who have ever lived in Greene County.

During my retirement, Winnie invited me to say "a word" at his funeral. My presentation was an open letter to Francis.

My days at Hendrix opened horizons that I had never dreamed existed. While I did not participate in varsity sports, except softball, I was "big" on intramural sports, encouraged by Francis, who remembered the score of certain games and exactly what happened and why. Those of us living on the fourth floor north of Martin Hall named ourselves "The Gas House Gang", after the St. Louis Cardinals. We bought ourselves red T-shirts with a skull and crossbones printed on the front.

The Gas House Gang participated in all intra-mural sports, touch football, basketball, hockey, boxing, etc. We did very well in hockey and touch football, as I remember. One year we won the championship in hockey. I played goalie on the hockey team. That was because I couldn't skate very well. Francis was a good player and kept the opponents from hitting me too hard too often. Lest you think otherwise, I must be quick to say that we did not play hockey on ice. We played it on the basketball floor of the old Axley Gym, on roller skates, using a wooden puck. It was rough, so rough that Coach Grove (Grovie) would not allow his varsity football players to participate, for fear they might get hurt. We did not have the protective pads worn by modern hockey players. I taped bamboo strips to the backs of the fingers on an old pair of work gloves. A chest protector (baseball type) was my protection from the fast flying wooden puck. I used a fencing mask to protect my face, and used shin guards for the obvious purpose.

Touch football was also a very rough game as we played it. The only difference between regular football and touch football was the way in which the ball carrier was stopped. No tackling was allowed. Touch the carrier and he was down. But blocking was a very important part of the game. Moreover, we played the game without any kind of protective pads.

Francis liked to tell about the championship game which the Gas House Gang played against a team made up of students who lived off campus. I ought to be able to tell this tale without missing a beat, since Francis has repeated it so often across the years, but I will be brief. We were ahead, barely, but deep in our own end of the field. In the last minute of the game our punter backed out of the end zone, and we lost by that safety. Francis was our passer. I played left end and caught the ball sometimes. Well, we had a very good thing going. It was good enough that the opposing team told one of their players, Byron Cravens (later to be my seminary room mate), to block me when I left the line of scrimmage, so I wouldn't have a chance to catch the ball. He succeeded in this a good deal of the time, but was frustrated when he failed.

Francis and I were playing linebacker in one of our touch football games. The offensive team threw a pass right between the two of us. Both of us, thinking we could intercept the pass, arrived at the same spot simultaneously. The collision sent Francis to the infirmary. Years later he complained of loose teeth, but his joy in retelling this episode has somewhat offset the inconvenience. Hendrix didn't have a baseball team in the thirties, but it did have a varsity softball team, fast pitch. Francis and I played on that team. I played roving shortstop most of the time, didn't have the arm for the outfield. Francis played shortstop, I think. We were fair players. If the pitcher made the mistake of pitching me a change up, I could knock the ball out of the park. Francis was a more consistent hitter.

Francis liked to tell about the time we were playing Arkansas State College at Jonesboro. There was a lumber pile way out in left field. A player on the Jonesboro team hit a ball into that lumber pile, and while our fielder was trying unsuccessfully to get the ball out, the runner just kept running, maybe scored. Francis thought there ought to have been some ground rule that would have helped our team. I agree.

Boxing was not for me, but Francis insisted that the Gas House gang had to have a participant in my weight. So, against my better judgment, I consented to represent the floor. My opponent turned out to be Bobby Weeks, a varsity football player. He beat the daylights out of me. One of his many blows hit me just above the right eye. The resulting cut began bleeding, so the ref stopped the fight. What a relief! Francis fought Byron Cravens in one match. I can't remember who won, but Francis never got me in the ring again.

I like to think that the Gas House Gang made a significant contribution to the establishment of intermural sports as an important part of the extracurricular activities at Hendrix. I am sure we helped to popularize intermural sports thru our fierce competitive spirit. One year we hired an airplane to fly over the campus at noon, when all the students were gathered outside the dining hall, to drop leaflets which told of a game to be played that afternoon. As the plane circled, someone turned on an air-raid siren. It created a great deal of excitement and assured a heavy attendance at the game. I heard that the varsity coaching staff complained that more students attended the intermural games than attended the varsity games. I never counted.

Financing my attendance at Hendrix was not an easy matter. Mother did not have the money to pay my way, so I had to work and borrow. Mrs. Viola Schilling Stone, one of my high school teachers, made it possible for me to borrow money from time to time. These were not long term loans. They were usually repaid in a few months. I appreciated this help very much and I hope that I expressed it promptly to my beloved teacher.

The North Arkansas Conference, under the leadership of Dr. Ira Brumley, had adopted a program which would let ministerial students work during the summers for money to be applied to their expenses at Hendrix in the fall. I think I earned $400 for eight or ten weeks of work in local churches across the conference. This was a tremendous help. I did this work for four summers. The money for this program was raised by a special offering taken once a year in the churches of the conference. Many ministerial students were enabled to get an education at Hendrix because this program was working.

One summer I was invited to preach a revival at Turner Methodist Church, a rural church near Marvell, Arkansas. Bro. A. N. Storey, pastor of the church, and I arrived at the Turner family home on a Sunday afternoon. This was the home in which we had been invited to stay during the meeting. We were met by Mr. Turner, who explained that his wife was away for the afternoon, because they had not expected us until after the evening service. Therefore, no supper was in view. Taking out a knife, Mr. Turner said, "Here is a knife; there is the peach tree. Go get your supper." We did.

After I retired in 1984, I was invited to Marvell, Arkansas, to preach on a Sunday morning. Following the worship service, I was invited by a family to go home with them for Sunday dinner. (That's a practice I wish had not disappeared). They lived a few miles out in the country. I knew the name of my host was Turner, but not until we had talked for some time at the dinner table did I make any connection with the Turners of the long-ago peach supper. Nor had my host made the connection. What I discovered was uncanny. My host was the son of the Mr. Turner who had invited us to the peach orchard for supper. They have told that story over and over again across the sixty years and more since that memorable Sunday afternoon.

No one today is very concerned about polio, but one summer while working at the Methodist Church in Ash Flat, Arkansas, I was really scared. Dr. Salk had not yet discovered the vaccine which would erase polio as a scourge of the people. A number of cases of polio had been diagnosed in that town, but I was sent to hold a revival there. Whether the health risk was known or not known to those who sent me, I never knew. Brother Luther Love was the pastor. It was depression time. Money for preaching was scarce. Bro. Love had been paid about twenty or thirty dollars in cash during the previous three months. I was to eat most of my meals with the pastor's family. We ate a lot of tomatoes! I remember that there were a number of Campbellites in that community who were known for their propensity to argue religion. In the barber shop one day I had an encounter with one of them. He took me to task for every Methodist belief. However, he mostly wanted to argue that his church was the only church and that baptism by immersion was the only Biblical mode. I knew then, as I know now, that it wasn't easy for me to tolerate people who were too sure of their position, hard for me to tolerate intolerance.

The government had a program which paid students for working on college campuses. I think they called this program NYA, National Youth Act. So, I raked leaves and did other yard work on the campus for twenty cents an hour. I know I raked enough leaves to fill the Superdome! Later I got a job as janitor in the science hall, now called Reynolds Hall, for Hendrix president John Hughes Reynolds. That job was better. It paid by the job, not by the hour, and I could work it into my schedule.

My main job on campus was working in Hulen Dining Hall. I started as a waiter making about nineteen cents a meal. This did not quite cover the board of $19.00 a month. However, occasionally I could set tables at sixteen and two thirds cents a "setting". (A "setting" consisted of placing table clothes and silverware, plates and glasses on six tables seating eight persons each. So, most of the time I made enough to pay my board. When Ewing Wayland graduated, I became the head waiter. I can't remember how much I made (maybe 21 cents a meal), but it was enough to pay my board and perhaps a bit more. This was one of the choice jobs for students on campus, and I was grateful for it. E. W. Martin was business manager of the college. Mrs. Georgia Hulen was the dietician. Miss Katherine Gaw was the dining room hostess. I am grateful to these persons for all the help and advice they gave me.

Late in my college career, I entered campus politics and was elected president of the student body for my senior year (1939-40). My opponent, Jimmie Christian, appeared in front of the dining hall after the election carrying a shotgun. It was a gesture of good sportsmanship. He said, on being asked, "Why the shotgun?": "If you didn't have any more friends than I have, you'd carry a gun, too." Jimmy was a splendid person who, across the years, has made a significant contribution to the things that matter.

Byron Cravens and I met two girls at First Methodist Church. We flipped a coin to see who would invite which young person to a Mt. Petit Jean hay-ride being sponsored by the church's youth group. Professor Caple from Hendrix was the sponsor. I won the blonde and Byron got the red head. I don't think Byron ever dated the red head after that, but I dated the blonde for about three years. She was a student at Teacher's College (now UCA), lived in town, was a year ahead of me in school, and a year older. We "broke up" and I began dating a Hendrix student in my senior year, Elizabeth Ann McQuistian.

But all at Hendrix was not fun and games and work. There were courses to be taken, for was not this the purpose of college? I wish I could say that I was a straight "A" student. I wasn't. However, I would have been eligible for graduation with honors, if it had not been for that string of "C's" I got in French. I did very well in the courses of my major, Philosophical Studies. In those "good ole days" Hendrix divided its curriculum into three divisions: Natural Sciences, Social Sciences, and Philosophical Studies. There were departments under these divisions. A student could major in a division or in a department. As I remember it, my Philosophical Studies Major included philosophy, Bible, psychology, and education. My major professor was Dr. Matt L. Ellis who shaped my thinking more than any other professor at Hendrix. I think it was the natural sciences that about "did me in". I am not talking about grades; I did very well in these courses. I am talking about the broad impact of these courses on my Christian faith.

I arrived at Hendrix as a ministerial student with a very conservative theology, except perhaps for my pacifism. When I began to see the evidence that the earth was much older than I had thought, that the universe was much bigger than I had thought, that man had almost certainly evolved from lower life forms, and that we need not take the Bible literally at all points, I had a crisis of faith. During my sophomore year, it seemed to me that I had to choose between science and religion, that I couldn't believe **both** about the way the world and man came into being. I struggled with this, and doubted my faith at times. Gradually, however, I developed a theology which could exist comfortably with science. Later I learned that this was "liberalism".

Dr. C. J. Greene, Dr. Nat Griswold, and Dr. Matt Ellis were my teachers in Bible, Religion, and Philosophy. They were the ones who helped me reconcile the differences which I saw between the conservative faith I brought with me to Hendrix and the new knowledge I was acquiring. While seminary and subsequent years of service as a pastor have corrected some aspects of my liberalism, I have remained essentially a liberal to this day. When a new and Republican daughter-in-law asked, some years ago, if I were a "bleeding heart liberal", I answered, "yes". She had not arrived at that conclusion because of theology, but because of the social views which I had expressed, views which usually accompany liberal views of God, Christ, man, society, and the world.

All thru my four years at Hendrix, I was a pacifist, an active and vocal one. Several of the ministerial students, and a few others, agreed with the pacifist position, although the "war spirit" was on the rise. Looking back on my nonviolent position today, I see it as just another attempt to earn my salvation by "works". I still could not sing, "In my hand no price I bring."

I am quite aware that theological, social, and political liberalism is not a popular position today. (Mild statement.) I do not expect a return by churchmen to classical liberalism; but, I believe that in the future there will be a blending of liberal and conservative views which more and more people will come to believe.

Here are examples:

1. Jesus was fully human and fully divine.

2. God is fully immanent as well as fully transcendent, always love and always just, always right here and always beyond reach.

3. Humankind possesses both a bent toward goodness as well as badness.

4. "Sainthood" is recognized in how we treat others as well as how we treat God.

5. From those who are given much, much is required, whether the recipients "deserve" it or not.

6. Respect for those who are different is both an admirable admission of inadequacies and a requisite for survival

7. Just because the poor are with us always, we are not excused from helping them.

8. Just because the Bible is God's Word, does not mean it is a science textbook and is without human characteristics.

9. Just because we are saved by faith, we are not released from "good works".

10. Somehow conviction, and tolerance must go hand in hand. They are not mutually exclusive.

I cannot over-state the importance of Hendrix College to the growth of my body, mind, and spirit. That is why I have tried to give her every means of support for all the days of my life thus far.

This does not mean that I agree with all that happens on the campus. (1) I do not think everything that can be done is being done to discourage the use of alcohol by students. (2) And, I don not think the degree of supervision in college housing adequately supports "celebacy in singleness", as the *United Methodist Book of Discipline* puts it.

Moreover, I am remembering a bit of the history of Hendrix, how the city of Conway had to be voted "dry" before Hendrix could be located in Conway. I am aware that the county is still "dry" legally, except for an "oasis" or two; i.e., country clubs, restaurants, etc., the number growing each year.

But my disagreement with these "inadequacies"of the college will not keep me from supporting Hendrix. It is a splendid educational institution. Our family has established a Paul and John Cooper Scholarship to which all the family contributes from time to time. And Bill and I belong to the President's Club, a list of donors who give a designated amount each year to Hendrix's alumni fund.

Robert Arbaugh, with whom I was licensed to preach in the Paragould District Conference, Oct. 1932, Rector, Arkansas, was three years ahead of me in Hendrix. He had gone on to Duke School of Religion for his theological training. I think this is the reason I settled on Duke as my first choice, along with the fact that Duke offered financial help thru its Duke Endowment program for summer work in rural North Carolina churches.

Having finished Hendrix, I was set to go to seminary, the last important step in my preparation for professional ministry. I went with good undergraduate foundations, as I was soon to discover.

7

"Inching along like a Four-inch Worm"

The aroma of tobacco filled the air as I disembarked from the train at the station in Durham, North Carolina, that September day in 1940. I learned later that this pungent smell resulted from large fans blowing air across the barrels of tobacco aging in the many warehouses. Not many people in those days considered the use of tobacco to be a serious health hazard. The Methodist Church frowned on its use by its ministers, but many ministers smoked anyway. Chewing and dips were not popular habits among ministers. It was in this environment that I became a regular smoker. I had fooled with this habit for several years, smoking a pipe some while at Hendrix, and a Red Dot cigar at times, but I never became a habitual smoker until seminary days at Duke. We often laughed and said, "We must support the company." We were referring to the fact that the Duke tobacco interests had established Duke University.

I continued to smoke until October of 1945, although I felt conscience-stricken by the practice. The North Arkansas Annual Conference was meeting in Walnut Ridge, and the night I was ordained Elder, I had a package of cigarettes in my coat pocket. Something happened to me as the bishop and elders placed their hands on my head and the bishop said, "Take thou authority, etc. " I knew that, as a Methodist minister, I was not supposed to smoke. But not until that moment of ordination did I find the motivation to quit "cold turkey". On returning to my mother's house in Paragould, twenty miles away, I dropped the pack of cigarettes into her coal burning stove. That was the last tobacco I would ever burn. However, I missed the cigarettes for a long time. More than once after a good meal I would say, "Oh, what I would give for a cigarette, a foot long, with whipped cream on it." No question about it, tobacco is addictive. Most admit it now.

When I went to Duke in the fall of 1940, I was "going steady" with Elizabeth Ann McQuistion who was in her senior year at Hendrix. I gave her an engagement ring. But "courting" long distance was difficult, and proved to be impossible in the end. I broke the engagement. For a few months I dated a student nurse in the Duke School of Nursing, but this did not last. She broke it off. I did no more serious dating, until I met Billie Charlene Thacker while attending Pastor's School at Hendrix in the summer of 1944.

You must understand that I arrived at Duke with a very liberal religious background, having discovered this liberating position at Hendrix College where I had majored in philosophic studies. Biblical criticism was nothing new to me as I entered my first classes at Duke, so I was not shocked, as some of my classmates **were**, at this approach to the Bible. Still the neo-orthodox reaction to liberalism which I found at Duke challenged me.

As a liberal, I had great confidence in humankind. I really believed that with the proper Christian training and discipline a person could become what God wants him/her to become. Didn't Wesley teach something like this? The social implication of this is clear: things were going to get better and better, the Kingdom of God, like prosperity, was just around the corner. It was this naive optimism about the nature of man that inspired the comment from Dr. Sheldon Smith, my Christian ethics professor, that the liberal position is described by the words, "'Inchin' along like a Four-Inch Worm; Massa Jesus is coming by and by." As he said it, he would crook his fore-finger like the movement of a measuring worm. My Duke days, and World War II, changed my mind. I began to see that sin was much more deeply rooted in man than I had thought, that humankind cannot pull itself up, morally speaking, by its own boot straps. Moreover, I began to see, dimly at first, that human salvation really depended upon the grace of God, not the efforts of man, however splendid. This change in theological direction was not a return to the total depravity position of some earlier theologians. Nevertheless, it was the adoption of a view of man which seemed to me to fit the experiences thru which we were passing in that historical moment when German planes were bombing London every night or so and rumors of Nazis gas chambers were rampant. I really think that this change in my view of the nature of man is the cause of my turn away from the pacifism I had tried to follow since the Christmas youth conference in Memphis. This change was not something that took place instantaneously. At the time, I could hardly realize it was happening. However, looking back, I know it was happening, that from that time on I would not expect too much from man. That did not mean that I had lost all faith in what man could accomplish toward "bringing in the Kingdom"; it meant that man **could** not do this task alone. That "realistic" view colored my preaching and action from that time to the present.

Moreover, as a liberal I had a view of God which could be classified as "immanent", I suppose. Of course, God is "nearer than breathing and closer than hand and foot', but as a liberal I saw God as almost identical with my environment. He was a part of creation. I drew Him into my inner circle. It was a "buddy-buddy" relationship that I had with God. Someone has called this a "deadening familiarity with the sublime." It's making this song our theme song: "And He walks with me, and He talks with me, etc."

What I began to see at Duke was that God was far more transcendent than I had thought. He was not a part of the world, a part of creation. He stood outside it, was Creator of the world, separate from it, the Mysterious Provider, as Dr. Albert Outler said in a later book. In some way which defies our understanding, God is IN the world but not OF the world. This understanding of God sees Him as awesome, majestic, mysterious, not fully knowable, not manageable by human endeavor, sees Him as a proper object of our worship. "His ways are not our ways" is the Biblical way of stating it. This emphasis upon the transcendence of God has colored my preaching and action from Duke days until now.

Moreover, as a liberal I viewed Jesus as a bit more human than divine. I could talk honestly about Jesus as the Son of God, but in any discussion of his nature I tilted toward his humanity. I wouldn't have said that Jesus was "just a man", as the musical "Jesus Christ, Superstar" says, but I leaned in this direction. It seemed to make more sense to me.

At Duke Divinity School in the beginning days of the 40's, I began to see that Jesus was more divine than I had thought. My studies covered the struggle of the early church to solve this mystery of Jesus' nature, and I saw the wisdom of the historic position that Jesus was both human and divine, "fully God and fully man". More and more often I looked to the verse, "God was **in** Christ reconciling the world unto Himself." I think the following statement is original: "God became one of us to get next to us." God poured Himself into a fully human person to accomplish what He had been trying to accomplish; i.e., a better way of salvation. God had tried the Law, the Prophets, but they had not worked as well as He wanted. So, "in the fullness of time", "He", as Dr. Caldwell once put it, "walked down the steps of heaven with a baby in His arms." Mysterious? Yes! But in the years at Duke I learned to live with this mystery. This makes it much easier to preach Jesus as Lord and Savior.

Some professors at Duke School of Religion, which I entered the fall of 1940, were reacting against the extremes of liberalism. It was the time when Reinhold

Niebuhr published his two volume work on "The Nature and Destiny of Man". It fell my assignment to report in class on these two volumes. I can't say that I understood all Niebuhr wrote, but I know that he influenced my life for good. He helped bring me around to a position which I feel is balanced on questions of the nature of man, God, and Jesus.

Dr. Albert Outler, Dr. Shelton Smith, Dr. Ray Petrie, Dr. Frank Hickman, Dr. Harvey Branscomb, Dr. Elbert Russell, Dean Garber, Dr. Steinspring were a few of the professors who made my stay at Duke such a rewarding experience. I feel that I was the fortunate recipient of one of the best opportunities in the nation to get a splendid theological education. Across the years as I prepared to preach, I felt the kibitzing influence of these men. In essence, almost verbally, I asked myself, "Would this point or that development or those facts be acceptable to my professors?" While I do not follow every detail of the Hickman method of preparing a sermon, his teaching has been invaluable.

Years later, I got the reputation of always having three points in my sermons. And that was largely true. I sometimes defended the three-point sermon by comparing a sermon to a stool. A stool with three legs can rest securely on most any surface. But a stool with four legs will not be secure on an uneven surface. One leg will always be off the floor. And, of course, a two-leg stool won't stand up by itself anywhere. So with sermons.

Dr. Hickman, my homiletic professor, told his students that his method was not the only method that could be used in preparing sermons, but that he wanted to teach us at least one method of doing it. He stuck with it, demanding that sermons must be outlined in very meticulous ways, indenting two spaces here and four spaces there, etc. Moreover, the outline was to be done on a special sized paper with a heavy black line down the left-hand margin. We theologs called it Hickman paper. More important was his insistence on writing out the purpose of the sermon, i.e., what we hoped to accomplish by it, etc.

While I have not achieved the level in doctrinal matters which Albert Outler held before me, I cannot possibly overstate my debt to him. It was a great joy, after I began working at Hendrix following my retirement, to invite him to Hendrix to give a lecture. He was retired, but continued to lecture and write. I will write more about this later.

Dr. Sheldon Smith was the Duke professor under whom I majored in Christian Ethics. There is no way I could exaggerate the importance of his teaching on my theological development. He allowed me to write my thesis on "The Nature and Mission of Jesus in the Thought of Henry Churchill King", a liberal theologian of the early twentieth century. But Sheldon Smith took me beyond liberalism. I have not become neo-orthodox or conservative. I still am liberal in my methodology and in many other ways. I do not have a name for my present theological position. Maybe I am too inconsistent to be labeled anything. That doesn't worry me. I felt complimented when a member of Grace UMC said to me, "I don't know whether you are a liberal or a conservative." I am an ethical conservative; i.e., I believe in the traditonal ethical values, the Ten Commandments, if you please. I am a conservative in that I accept the traditional theology of John Wesley. I am a liberal in the way in which I talk about some of the traditional theology. For example, I have said that I believe God became man in Christ Jesus, but I don't think a person has to believe in the Virgin Birth of Jesus to believe that Jesus was divine. From my perspective, a person can believe in the Virgin Birth or not believe in it. Maybe that **is** the way God became man. I don't know. Not all the writers of the gospels record the virgin birth. This is not an issue for me. What is basically important to Christianity is the faith that God became man in Christ Jesus. However, since I believe there is a spirit world beyond this one of time and space, I do not think it is outside the realm of reason or faith to accept the virgin birth at face value.

Here is another example of this liberal way of talking about conservative things: I believe that Jesus is "the way, the truth, and the life." But I do not believe that all persons who do not accept this are lost. A merciful God must somehow love sincere followers of other religions. If I am involved in a logical absurdity, so be it. What I know is: in this next century we are going to live very close to members of non-Christian religions. I do not think we can live peaceably in a pluralistic and shrinking world and think that we are the only ones God cares about.

Right now the UMC is divided along some of these lines. Members of the church are being pressured to take a side, to be a liberal or a conservative. I think that the way out of this problem is to be found in looking at liberal ways of talking about conservative ideas. I have a feeling that there is a core of belief in which both liberals and conservatives agree, that the disagreement is often in the way in which the core beliefs are expressed and emphasized.

In the first two years at Duke, I wrote articles for a student magazine entitled *"Christian Horizons"*. As I read some of these later, I realized how poorly they were done. In my last year, I was elected editor of the publication, a position of some honor. I did not make the highest grades in Duke. As I remember, we could receive three grades: Excellent, Satisfactory, and Failing. I don't remember making an "F", and I made a good many "E's". All in all, I did satisfactory work, good enough to get a scholarship to do graduate work beyond the BD degree.

It was during my oral examination on my thesis that Dr. Albert Outler asked me a question I could not answer. He looked at me and said, "Joel, you had better know the answer to that question by the time you take my exam in Church Doctrine." I had not been doing the required reading for the course I was taking under him, spending most of my time on my thesis. But I can tell you that when the exam came, I did know the answer. Dr. Outler remembered his warning to me, and mentioned it as he returned my paper.

Office space must have been short in the ad building, for Dr. Sheldon Smith moved his office to a dorm room next to the room which I shared with Byron Cravens. The students in the medical school lived on the same floor with the divinity students, used the same shower rooms. After the medics had finished a round of examinations, they celebrated, leaving an almost empty whiskey bottle in the shower room. Some divinity student picked up the bottle, brought it to my room with the comment, "Look what the docs left in the bathroom." He put the bottle down on my study table. It stayed there for several days, but one day I said, "Let's get this bottle out of here before someone sees it and thinks it is ours." So, a friend in our room picked up the bottle and started for the door. There was a knock on the door. My friend opened the door with one hand while holding the bottle with the other. There stood Dr. Smith. He had come to ask some question and never seemed to see the compromising situation. Mercy!

My first year at Duke, I worked in the Cary Methodist Church, Cary, N. Carolina, just a few miles east of Durham toward Raleigh. The Duke Endowment program funded the work. The second and third years I was the pastor of Eno Methodist Church near Hillsboro, N. Carolina. Eno was a mill village. Many houses were owned by the textile mill, and most of the adult, able-bodied people worked in the mills. The working conditions were not good and not bad. By some earlier standards and some other places, the workers did well. But the high humidity in the mill, required for textile work, took its toll in upper respiratory illnesses.

One summer I had a room and boarded with an elderly couple who took me under their wing, treating me as a member of the family. She made a wonderful Brunswick stew, the first I had ever eaten. I remember that she cooked it all day long it in a big black pot outdoors. Brunswick stew church suppers were common in that part of North Carolina.

One summer In the 1950's when our family on vacation was visiting Duke, we drove to Eno where I had been the pastor. I told my family, "If the couple is still living, at this time of day they will be sitting on their front porch." We drove to the house, and sure enough, there they sat. They invited us into the front room and took the boys, Paul, Marc, Chris, and Clay, to a side table on which she kept my picture. It had been there, maybe ten years. Bill said that I had bragged on the Brunswick stew all across the years and that she wanted the recipe. The two of them gave Bill the recipe from memory, e.g., "Cook two fat hens, etc."

I will never forget December 7, 1941; nobody of my generation can. I was about to begin the worship service at Eno when someone came up to me in the pulpit and whispered, "The Japanese have bombed Pearl Harbor." I hate to admit that I did not even know where Pearl Harbor was, but I realized that it was a serious situation. At that time I did not know how serious!

Forty years later, while attending the World Methodist Conference in Honolulu, Bill and I took a tour of Pearl Harbor and saw the water graveyard of the many Americans lost that fateful day. I had some problem feeling courteous toward the Japanese who were on the same tour.

The church at Eno, N.C. (a part of Hillsboro) paid me $100 a month, perhaps one-half of this coming directly from the mill company. I remember that the company wanted me to come and get my check like the other workers. However, this rubbed me the wrong way, so I arranged to receive the check by mail. I will not try to analyze my feelings about this matter. The pay was adequate for my needs, and when I left Duke to return to Arkansas in the fall of 1943, I had enough money to pay my income tax and get home. I had finished four years of college and three years of seminary work and did not have a debt—financial, that is.

A funny but serious, even stupid, incident I must now relate. As I have said, I was a pacifist in my early days at Duke. Pacifists were suspect, and the School of Religion, having several pacifists among its students, was being viewed with a jaundiced eye by some professors and the university administration. It was George Washington's birthday. The school was holding a tea in celebration. The flags of the Allies were prominently displayed in the room. For some reason, which I cannot understand to this day, two or three of us took a handkerchief, drew a "rising sun" and a swastika on it, and left it among the other flags. It was just a prank, but we should have known better, given the mood of the times. The proverbial "hornet's nest" was stirred. Rumor had it that there were collaborators in the School of Religion. The handkerchief we used had the laundry mark of one of my friends. This mark was traced and they called my friend on the carpet. When we heard of this, another friend and I were unwilling for the identified friend to carry the full blame. We went before the dean, confessed, and received our deserved reprimand. A well-known scholar and professor in the School of Religion wanted to know "What made you do such a damn fool thing?" We were never able to get him to accept the "harmless prank" argument. He knew we should have known better. Unless you had been there, you cannot imagine how raw the nerves of people can get in wartime.

Thirty years later they invited me to give the alumni address at the annual Duke Divinity School Convocation. A fellow student of mine, then on the faculty, was about to tell the story of the mixed flags as a part of his introduction of me before my lecture. But just in time, he spotted a professor, long time retired, sitting near the front of the auditorium, the same professor whom our "prank" many years before had disturbed. Obviously, my friend did not open old wounds.

The lecture was well received, I thought. They reprinted it in the divinity school journal and at least one Methodist journal, but shortly after my lecture they deleted this feature from the convocation schedule. I have said that I was "the straw that broke the camel's back."

After graduating with a B.D. degree from Duke Divinity School (the name had changed while I was there), I applied for and received a scholarship to do further graduate work, and I attended classes during September and October. But I was tired after nineteen straight years of schooling, and the war continued. It did not seem quite right to be in school when so many were giving so much to the war effort. So, I went to see the dean of the graduate school one day and told him that I wanted to go back to Arkansas and take a charge. He figured a little and said, "Your expenses about equal your scholarship. What do you say to calling it even?" So, I left Duke without debt ready to take whatever the bishop and the cabinet of the North Arkansas Conference would give me. And they did give it to me—a six point circuit in Cross County.

8

Six Ring Circus

When I asked for a pastoral appointment in the North Arkansas Conference, I bared my bosom, agreeing to accept whatever resulted. That is the "trade off" in the United Methodist way of making appointments. A fully accredited minister is assured of a job if he behaves himself and does "fair-to-medlin" work. In all my forty years as a minister I never knew the pain of "involuntary" unemployment.

In November of 1943, they "read me out" to the Vanndale-Cherry Valley Charge, towns in Cross County, Arkansas, and I would live in a parsonage at Vanndale, just two houses from the church building. It was a modest four-room frame house with "running water"; i.e., I would grab a bucket, run to the neighbor's well, draw the water, and run back. That was our drinking water. Other water came from a cistern. We had a hand-operated pitcher pump in the kitchen. We described the parsonage as "four rooms and a path"; i.e., a path to the "outhouse". A large coal burning stove in the front room was the only source of heat for the entire house. When I lived there before I married, to keep warm, I put the bed in the front room, but when I married, we moved the bed to the bedroom. Even with the warmth of a new bride, I remember how cold it was. I slept in my "long handles". All the floors in the house were covered with linoleum which made for rapid movement of any bare feet.

There was a crank-operated telephone on the wall close to the front door. To place a call, I would lift the receiver and give the crank a couple of quick turns. An operator would answer with the customary, "Number please." Telephone numbers could be found in the little telephone book tied with a string to the telephone, but more often than not I would answer": "Ring Jim for me", or "ring Charlie". Numbers were not necessary because the local switchboard had only forty or so subscribers and the operator knew them all by memory. The local switchboard operator was Mrs. Laney who ran a boarding/rooming house and tended the switchboard on the side, or the other way around. I boarded with her, so she knew me and my business very well. One day when I was talking on my home phone, making some kind of appointment, Mrs. Laney broke into the conversation to remind me that I had a conflict with the appointment being discussed. No one thought very much about Mrs. Laney's listening to the calls which came thru her switchboard, for her knowledge of what was going on in the community was invaluable. Anyone could ring the switchboard and find out what was happening. Sometimes when I arrived early for a meal at Mrs. Laney's, she would ask me to tend the switchboard while she did final preparations for the meal. I would put on the headphones and wait for the calls. When a patron rang the switchboard, which was on a vertical panel in front of me, a little door would fall down revealing the number of the person calling. I would plug in that number and do my thing: "Number, please." I soon learned how to connect the caller with "Jim" or "Charlie", but had to have the number for the other patrons. When the number was given, I would make the necessary plug in connections, turn the ringer, and wait until someone answered, or didn't. Then I would disconnect from the conversation. I do not remember listening in.

Mealtime at the Laney boarding house was a pleasant experience, not only because of the quality of the food—very good, but the quality of the conversations. A number of the boarders were school teachers who discussed many things in which I had an interest. Then there were the drop-ins, not regular boarders. They brought interesting accounts of what was going on in farming. There were the discussions about the progress of the war.

The dessert was always a subject of interest and discussion for the boarders at Mrs. Laney's. She did not put the dessert on the table at the beginning of the meal but kept it hidden behind a panel in the kitchen. The inevitable question was: "What's behind the board?" To this day, that question is still asked in the Cooper family when we want to know what's for dessert.

I had picked up the habit of smoking while at Duke. Not smoking was difficult, for the very air of Durham was saturated with the smell of tobacco, a condition caused by the big exhaust fans in the warehouses. I continued to smoke while at Vanndale. Tailor-made cigarettes were not easy to buy. "Lucky Strike Green had gone to war." However, the clerks in the grocery store always kept a few packages "under the counter".

They inducted a friend from Vanndale into the army and he was soon in the Pacific area. I dreamed one night that he had been wounded. I could just see him holding the back of his neck and saying, "Oh, it's nothing." I was surprised, on opening my box at the post office, to get a card from him that very day saying that he had been wounded in the neck, and that it was not serious. I had learned about ESP, etc. and the work of Dr. Ryan, while at Duke, where experiments in these matters had drawn wide recognition. Am I clairvoyant? I doubt it, for I have never had an experience like that again. Well, maybe once more. Tell you later.

Not long after my appointment to the six-point circuit, which I often called a "six-ring circus", I began to have unexplained pain in my right side, just beneath the breast bone. I ended up in the hospital at Wynne, county seat of Cross County, just six miles away. The doctor said I had a diseased gall bladder, and added, "I can patch you up, but this pain will return, unless you have the gall bladder removed." So, I went to the Methodist Hospital in Memphis to have this work done. I really didn't know the seriousness of a colosistectomy. Of course, it is done on an out-patient basis today, but small incision surgery was not practiced then. I am sure I was more anxious than I should have been, but as I approached the surgery, I said a prayer: "O God, I am prepared to do ministry for you. If you want me to continue, fine. If not, that's fine too." A peace came over me that I believe was of God. I left the hospital after three weeks. I found out later, that one nurse at the hospital was a cousin of the young lady I married. The nurse's name was Sue.

As I related in the previous chapter, I had "broken up" with the young woman from Hendrix before leaving Duke, and for reasons I do not fully understand. She returned the ring. The relationship with a Duke nurse did not pan out. I had a few dates with girls around Vanndale, Wynne, Paragould, but nothing serious developed, until I went to Pastor's School at Hendrix in June of 1944. It was there that I met the "pretty young thing" (just barely 19) who was to become my wife on November 7 of the same year. Her name was Billie Charlene Thacker, the only daughter of Charlie and Bevie Thacker of Danville, Arkansas.

Bill, as she was called by most of her friends and relatives (except her mother who insisted on calling her "Charlene"), was in her sophomore year at Hendrix. She was a Baptist and had been thinking about attending Ouachita Baptist College in Arkadelphia; but a friend from Danville, Katherine Ferguson, who was attending Hendrix, intervened. She "talked up" Hendrix to Bill and her father, convincing them that Hendrix was the college to attend.

On the first day of Pastor's School, June of 1944, I was walking across the campus with Everett Vincent. We met Bill and Mary Hoggard. I did not know then, but Mary had seen Everett and me before we met them. She said to Bill, (something like this) "There comes a young preacher I want you to meet. He may be taken, but … " And so Bill and I met, the introduction being made by Mary. Others have claimed, across the years, that they introduced the two of us. It pleases me now to think that several persons want to take credit for our meeting.

Bill and I dated frequently during the two weeks of Pastor's School. We saw each other every day during the last week, playing tennis, going to the worship services, etc. I skipped some classes to be with her, but I was about more important business. The teachers understood. I kissed Bill in the Hendrix War Memorial Stadium (long since demolished), and I asked her to marry me. I was ready to get married, but Bill needed to finish college. Now she tells me that I gave her the impression that if she didn't marry me, I would look elsewhere. She believed it, and not wanting that to happen, agreed in principle to my proposal. Nevertheless, no date was set.

I visited Bill at her home in Danville, and met her parents and a brother, all God-fearing, honest, hard-working Baptists. I should say that her father was not a member of the Baptist Church then. He had made a profession of his faith but had never been baptized. His baptism took place later in his life. He was an agent for the Conoco Oil Company, selling their products to filling stations, grocery stores, and farmers in Yell County—the "free state of Yell", as many called it. Bill's mother was typical of her times, i.e., she saw herself as wife, mother, and homemaker. She had taught school for several years in one-room school houses, but her primary concern in life was her family.

While I was visiting in Bill's home, her father and I got into a "deep"conversation about something. Bill's mother, Bevie, was in the kitchen fixing supper, but mindful of the conversation taking place in the front room. She whispered to Bill, "What are they talking about?" Bill answered, "I don't know, Mother." Bevie pursed her lips, nodded her head in an all-knowing fashion, and said: "Joel is asking Charlie for your hand in marriage." I don't think I was, but that remark was typical of her certainty that Bill would marry me. Turning to Bill, Bevie said, "When I was pregnant with you, I told the Lord that if he would give me a baby girl, I would raise her in the church." She did. While Bevie was a Baptist, she had been reared a Methodist, so that may be the reason she had no problem with her daughter marrying a Methodist preacher. Sometime during the courtship, but before the engagement, she said, "Charlie, Charlene is going to marry that preacher." I liked Bill's family.

Bill came to see my family in Paragould. My mother had married a widower, Ben McAden, five years after my father's death. He was the custodian at the Paragould Post Office, a fine man, a good churchman, the nephew of the preacher for whom they named the Griffin-Memorial United Methodist Church in Paragould. My mother loved Bill from the start. My sister, Nestel Woodward, lived in Paragould, worked as secretary of lst UMC. Bill and Nestel became lifelong friends. My brother, John, was in Paragould High School, playing the trumpet. Bill liked my family.

Bill returned to Hendrix in the fall of 1944, but our plans for marriage were developing rapidly. The date was set for November 7, right after the meeting of the North Arkansas Annual Conference in Morrilton. So Bill left school and went home to prepare for the marriage which would be held in the Methodist Church of Danville, the Rev. Herschell Couchman officiating.

Ordinarily, a wedding is held in the church of the bride, but I wanted to be married in a Methodist Church. Bill agreed, for theologically, she was more of a Methodist than a Baptist, and the Baptist preachers she had known were long gone. The Methodist pastor invited me to preach at the Sunday evening service on the day before the wedding. The attendance at this service was unusually good. Bill said later that they had all come out to see what the local girl had drug up. Bill was popular in Danville, having been selected as Yell County Queen in her senior year in high school. I don't remember my text, but I "took off" from the nursery rhyme, "Pussy cat, pussy cat, where have you been? I have been to London to see the Queen. Pussy cat, pussy cate, what saw you there? I saw a mouse under her chair."

Any kind of preacher could make a sermon out of that, for is it not true that we often begin our lives in a quest of high and noble things, but later settle for much less?

The night before the wedding, about twelve or one o'clock in the morning, I went to the depot to meet Byron Cravens, my Duke roommate who was coming from Oklahoma City to be my best man. I drove Mr. Thacker's car, because my old Plymouth, 1937 model, was packed with all of Bill's "stuff" we were to take to Vanndale. I parked the car at the depot facing the railroad track to await the arrival of the train. I went to sleep.

The train roared in, Byron got off, the train roared out, and I slept on. Byron, unable to find anyone to meet him, hitched a ride to Bills' house. Since no car was available to go to the depot or to look for me, Bill drove Byron in the gasoline truck. They found me still asleep in the car at the depot. This is a little embarrassing, but makes a good story.

It was election day and Charlie Thacker, Bill's father, was the township chairman, but he was so shy and modest that Bill did not know for sure that he would attend the wedding. Bill wore a blue suit. A long white dress with a veil was "just too formal and 'showy' for my dad." Only one bride in Danville had a formal church wedding, and she had offered Bill that dress. But, Charlie Thacker was so modest and quiet and "backward", that blue seemed more appropriate, and it certainly improved the chances of Charlie's attendance. Bill was just beautiful in blue, crystal buttons, a lacy blouse, etc..

Louise Thacker, Bill's sister-in-law, sang "O Perfect Love" and "Ah, Sweet Mystery of Life". Mrs. Maude Wilson played the piano. Bill's brother, Clayborne, gave the bride away. Bill and I took the Lord's Supper as a part of the ceremony, something not done often in those days at weddings. I bought the wedding license in Cross County, Arkansas.

It was cold and raining "cats and dogs", as we left Danville on our honeymoon. We drove the overloaded '37 Plymouth to Russellville and spent our first night together in a hotel. What happened in our hotel room was a first experience for both of us, so our clumsy moves were expected and tolerated. We managed.

The next day we drove to Petit Jean Lodge where we were to spend several days before going home to Vanndale. Being late in the tourist season, we were the only ones at the lodge. The host prepared wonderful meals for us, lobster etc. Bill said it was the best food she had ever eaten. Me too. So we ate and slept and explored the trails and each other. We still return to Petit Jean now and then and remember.

My salary on the Vanndale-Cherry Valley charge was $1,150 a year—not a month. It was not easy, even in those days, to "make it" on that salary. I had six churches on a circuit that was fifty miles around. No travel expense. True, as a preacher I had a "C" sticker which allowed me to buy more gas than most people, and gas was cheap, ten or eleven cents, but it was still difficult to "get by".

Once, when we were out of money, Bill worried. I told her that my mother had once said, "God will provide". The next day Mr. Lessenberry came by the house and paid "something on the preacher's salary." On that charge in those days the pastor did not receive a regular monthly salary check. When we moved from Vanndale, we did not owe anyone and had fifty dollars. We have often laughed and said, "And we have not been that well off since."

The farmers of Cross County were just beginning to grow rice. Some members of the church were rice farmers. It was before combines were widely used. Most communities did not have rice drying facilities, so the rice had to be cut, shocked, left in the field, and then thrashed when the thrashing crew got around to their farm. Sometimes the rain came before the thrashing crew arrived. The butts of the rice stalks were soaked and would not run thru the thrasher. So, before they threw the shocks of rice into the thrasher, they laid the shocks on a wooden block and cut off the butts with a broad axe. What a hard way to go! Now, of course, the rice is combined in the field and hauled to a dryer.

I was the only resident pastor of any denomination in Cross County outside the city of Wynne. Many part-time preachers worked in defense plants, lived away from the county, driving to their churches on Sunday. Therefore, I conducted many funerals of non-members of the Methodist Church. Sometimes I would have two funerals on the same Sunday afternoon. I remember one funeral in particular. I rode in the hearse along the graveled Highway l, north of Cherry Valley. We stopped at a muddy road leading east to a cemetery on Crowley's Ridge, about a mile or two away. The driver of the hearse knew he could not drive thru the mud, and had a contingency plan. A tractor hitched to a flat bed, rubber-tired trailer was waiting for us. We loaded the casket onto the flatbed trailer. Several of us got on the trailer and rode thru a sleet and rain storm across the "bottoms" to the cemetery on top of the ridge. Several dozen people had made it to the cemetery who had not attended the funeral. They wanted the casket opened. I looked into the grave which had about a foot of water in the bottom. No vault. It was a hard time, but these were hardy people, many of them scratching out a living on the poor clay soil atop the ridge. It may not have seemed like an ordeal to them, but to me it was rough.

It was fifty miles around my circuit, so I had to have some kind of transportation. The father of Francis Bland, my Hendrix College room mate, got word to me that he could buy me a 1937 model Plymouth in good condition. if I wanted it. He would let me borrow the money, $650. Remember that no new cars were available for civilian purchase. The war. I could play him back as I was able. I agreed and signed a note for the entire amount. At the end of the year I had saved $100 and Bill's father had given us $100 as a wedding present (plus thirty silver dollars which Bill had saved to buy a bicycle). I took the $230 to Mr. Bland and told him that it was all I could pay him then. This news did not seem to disturb him. He called out to his wife: "Elvira, bring me Joel's note." When he had the note in hand, he turned it over and wrote something on it and passed it to me. I read with disbelief, "Paid in full".

The bishop had assigned me in November of 1943 to six churches: Vanndale, Cherry Valley, Pleasant Hill, Farm Hill, Birdeye, and Bay Village. My preaching schedule for the first and third Sundays was as follows: Pleasant Hill at 9:30 A. M., Vanndale at 11: 00 A. M., Farm Hill at 2:30 P. M., Bay Village at 3:30 P.M., and Cherry Valley at 7:00 P. M. My schedule for the second and 4th Sundays: Birdeye at 9:30 A. M., Cherry Valley at 11:00 A. M., Vanndale at 7:00 P. M. Easy. I can't remember my schedule for the 5th Sundays which came quarterly.

Rice often means good duck hunting, and I found it with the help of friends in my Cherry Valley Church. They were glad to take the preacher hunting. One day when I was late for a hunt, they kidded me that I was late because I could not leave my new wife. They didn't know how right they were. The Languille River was not far away, and rice fields were all around. Noel Morris with a duck caller could make a duck ashamed of itself. So we hunted, and sat around the pot-bellied stove in the store in Cherry Valley and talked about the hunts that had been and were yet to come. During the war, buying new guns was difficult. Finally, I was able to buy a 12 guage Winchester pump.

Many years after these hunts, Bill and I were traveling one night thru Cherry Valley, heading toward Paragould. I said to Bill while looking at my watch, "If my hunting buddies are still alive, at this time of night they will be in the store around the stove." I stopped, and sure enough—there they were just like I had left them years before. Older, of course, but aren't we all?

I hunted quail as well as ducks. Lester Bledso, a farmer, my age, who raised sweet potatoes, took me on many enjoyable hunts. Sometimes I hunted alone. I had asked Bill to take me up into the hills behind the parsonage, and drop me off. I intended to hunt all the way back home.

We had a blind paper man. It was uncanny what he could do. Vanndale had no sidewalks, but he could make it from house to house delivering the papers. One day I left the car parked in a different place in the yard. When he ran into it, he whacked it with his cane and muttered something about people who leave their cars in the wrong place. I saw him one night by my car's headlights building a bridge in front of his home. He was at our house when we were ready to leave for the hunt, and we invited him to go for the ride. He was pleased and we chatted as we drove into the hills, making several turns. They dropped me and started back, but Bill made a wrong turn. Quickly, the blind man told her of her mistake, turned her around, and guided her back home. In this instance, the blind leading the blind did not result in both falling into the ditch.

I have mentioned the lack of facilities in the parsonage. We took baths in a number two galvanized tub situated usually in the middle of the kitchen floor. Bill was doing her absolutions one day in the tub when she heard the whistling of the iceman coming around the house to deliver the fifty pounds. She had just enough time to jump out of the tub and run to a nearby closet. The iceman came and went. When Bill crept cautiously from the closet, she saw that her wet feet had left clear tracks going from the tub to the closet, a dead give away. Were the tracks unobserved, or was the iceman just courteous?

It was during this period that the news came, "President Franklin Roosevelt has died." The allied forces were winning the war, but it was not over. Rev. Lyman Barger went into the chaplaincy leaving a vacancy. The pastor at Mt.

Home, J. J. Clark, moved to Lyman's church, and that left a vacancy at Mt. Home. In June of 1945 (between conference sessions at that time) I was appointed to Mt. Home Methodist Church.

9

Dam…. Dam

Mt. Home was my first "station" charge after seminary. That means that I was the pastor of only one church. But not for long. Soon I would be preaching in rural churches all around the town, churches that were no longer strong enough to pay a preacher.

Henry Goodloe was the District Superintendent of the Batesville District where Mt. Home was located. Dr. Goodloe was married to my mother's cousin. I do not know if this had anything to do with my appointment to Mt. Home, but it certainly didn't hurt my chances. Dr. G was a good superintendent, well grounded in the history and theology of The Methodist Church. He had been one of my teachers in that Pastor's School at Hendrix when I met Bill Thacker. Although I missed some classes, as I have said, he "passed" me anyway. For all the years of ministry after that, he remained a good friend who once said, "I would like to see you go to Pulaski Heights UMC one day." I didn't, of course, but it was a pleasant thought.

Bill and I packed our things, not many in those days, in her dad's pickup and the 37 Plymouth which we called "Shasta". (She has to have gas, shasta have oil, etc.) The pickup had side boards. I know that we looked like Steinbeck's "Okies" as we said goodbye to the wonderful people of the Vanndale-Cherry Valley Charge and started across north Arkansas to a place we had never seen in the Ozark mountains, Baxter County. It was to become our mountain home (a pun intended) for the next four and one half years.

We went thru Hardy and Ashflat and Salem, seeing mountains that we had not seen before, Bill driving Shasta and I driving the pickup. In the mountains west of Salem, Arkansas we came upon a scene that thrilled us enough to make us stop and look. Down in a valley below us was the bluest and biggest lake we had ever seen, Norfork. We did not know then how important that lake would be in our lives in the years to come; we just stood by Shasta and drank in the beauty.

I cannot remember if I knew about the Norfork ferry before we got to it, but it was exciting nevertheless. We had to wait for the ferry to come across from the west side, about two miles away. I think it left the east side on the hour and half hour. Later we learned how to time our arrival so that we could make it without much of a wait. Inevitably, sometimes, we arrived just as the ferry was pulling out from the shore.

This first ride across the lake on this ferry operated by the State Highway Department, which could carry maybe a dozen cars, was most enjoyable–a little nervous, perhaps. And then, we were on to Mountain Home, twelve or fifteen miles to the west.

The parsonage was an improvement over the one at Vanndale. Thank you, Lord! It had a bathroom with running water, not hot, but you could turn a faucet and fill the tub, and flush the commode. Later, Lew Park and I put in the plumbing necessary for the new propane gas water heater, kidding each other about the "nipples" we were using in the work.

The parsonage was next door to the church, a not uncommon placement in those days. Bill and I were not "sure" about this arrangement. It all came home to me that day when the quilting ladies from the church came in our back door, without knocking, to use the bathroom which was already in use at the time. I was fortunate enough to hear them chatting as they climbed the back stairs and barely had time to get decent. The church building was without a toilet, and it was common practice for church people to use the parsonage's facilities. Bill had been told by her friend, Eloise Hackler, to be sure to clean the bathroom every Sunday before Sunday School.

When we first arrived at this new home in June of 1945, we found a wood stove in the front room. It was adequate for the front room, but did not affect the other rooms. The cook stove was an old oil stove–old, that is. If you did not adjust the burners just right, it would smoke like a wood-burning steam locomotive. It was bound to happen, and did. Bill left the maladjusted demon alone in the closed kitchen for some time. When we finally entered, the light bulb hanging in the middle of the room looked like an orange suspended in the middle of the blackest night. The room was full of smoke and soot. The cleanup resulted in considerable wear on hands and tempers. However, we lived to see a new gas range in that place, wow! Was the upgrade the result of the eruption or was it because gas stoves, floor furnaces; etc., were again on the market, WWII shortages having ended? Yes, we got a propane floor furnace, too, and an electric refrigerator. Didn't we have it made? Bill said it was all because of Carl Keys, a leading layman and lumber man with connections, who was present with his wife on the Sunday of the kitchen "blackout".

It was during my pastorate at Mt Home that I was ordained elder in the Methodist Church. The annual conference met in Walnut Ridge, Arkansas that year—1945. Bishop Paul Martin and others laid their hands on my head, and said, "Lord, pour upon Joel the Holy Spirit for the office and work of an elder, in the name of the Father, and the Son, and the Holy Spirit. Amen."

As I knelt with hands laid upon me, I thought of the package of cigarettes in my coat pocket and determined that I would never smoke again. It was against the rules of the church for ministers to use tobacco, although they did not enforce the rule. After the service when I had arrived back at my mother's house in Paragould, I went to her coal stove and with some ceremony dropped the package of cigarettes into the fire. I have never smoked from that hour to this, Smokers who want to kick the habit must have the right motivation.

Having dealt with the unimportant things first, (Bill laughed when I read this to her) I now turn to our reason for being in Mt. Home; i.e., to serve the church. The church building was an attractive old structure which had been a Cumberland Presbyterian Church before the Methodists purchased it. This frame structure with an imposing tower, stood close to the main street running thru the town, about a block from the city square. It was adequate at first, but during the Year of Evangelism in the general church's Crusade for Christ, I received around 130 members, second in the conference to 1st UM Church Ft. Smith. Don't think for a minute that this achievement was the result of my skillful leadership. The war had ended and the soldiers were returning to take up their lives again. Hundreds of new people were arriving from Illinois and Indiana (Yankee land) to experience the mountains, the lake, the mild winters, etc., of what was to be one of the fastest growing areas in the state.

The primary method of evangelism in those days was door knocking, Visitation Evangelism. Church members were sent out two by two to visit in the homes of prospective members, some transfer prospects, some first time commitment prospects. Lola Park and Bill Cooper formed one team. I assigned them to a man who had "never darkened the door of the church," a difficult case, although his wife was at church every time the door was opened. Bill and Lola went thru the "seven and six" I had taught them, scared to death, because neither one had done this kind of work before. Afterwards the man told his wife that the girls made a pretty speech. Unfortunately, he never broke his record of church attendance, or lack of it.

As I said in the beginning of this chapter, I started conducting services in the rural churches around Mt. Home, developing what was we called the Mt. Home Larger Parish. Byron McSpadden, Methodist preacher about my age, was sent to be a co-pastor with me on this new work. We built a new parsonage for Byron and Irene and their son, Lynn. Together we worked in ten different communities, including Norfork and Gassville. I had primary responsibility for the Mt. Home Church and Byron had primary responsibility for the Norfork and Gassville Churches. But we shared the preaching and pastoring load of the other churches, some meeting in regular church buildings and some in school houses.

In the summer Byron and I attempted to have a week's revival in each of the ten churches. We ran the "meetings" from Sunday night thru Friday or Saturday nights. The North Arkansas Conference bought a surplus army hospital tent which we pitched in the various communities. The revivals held in these tents were fairly-well attended and several "conversions" took place.

One summer we were having a revival in the tent which we had set up on the Salesville school yard, about a mile below Norfork dam. Beside the pulpit was a tent pole. A kitten had followed someone to church that night. As I preached, it ran up and down the pole next to me. I thought, "The Holy Spirit surely cannot do its work with this kitten's playful antics taking front and center." But it did. A mature young man came forward and gave his heart to the Lord.

In that same meeting, one night I heard the sound of horses running. It got louder. The horses did not stop until they got into the light shining out from under the tent. There they began to chomp loudly on the grass. It didn't seem to bother the congregation very much, but it distracted me. What I discovered in these revivals was: the rural people of Baxter County were not really bothered by babies crying, boys going in an out, horses grazing, kittens playing, etc. Those disturbances which set my teeth on edge were not unusual for them.

Mrs. Lieb, a fine lady in the Mt. Home church, knowing the work which Byron and I had been doing in the rural communities, nominated me as Arkansas' Rural Minister of the Year. The Progressive Farmer magazine sponsored the program. My award was an expense paid, three week's special school on rural work held at Emory University. This was to be the longest time away from Bill in all our sixty plus years of marriage.

I enjoyed fishing on Lake Norfork, but I did not fish on Sunday. A barber who looked something like me, did, to my sorrow. Some of my members, fishing on Sunday, saw him and thought they were seeing their preacher. The next time I got a hair cut, I requested the barber to change his fishing days. One Sunday morning before Sunday School, there was a knock on the parsonage door. I opened it to find a friend standing there. He did not hesitate to ask me to let him borrow my minnow bucket. What? Should I react by "letting him have it", the bucket, that is? I did, reluctantly.

It was during these days that the war ended, and Joe Bill Hackler returned home to Mt. Home. Joe and I had been in Hendrix together, although he was a year or two ahead of me. Sometime before Joe's home coming, Eloise, his wife, had received the sad news that Joe was missing in action. I may not have every detail right, but, as I remember it, Joe's plane had taken a direct hit from anti-aircraft fire. Joe's parachute opened, he does not remember how, and he floated to the ground in enemy territory and was captured. Eloise did not know this at first. She was told in letters from Joe's friends, who were in another plane on the fateful mission, that no parachutes were seen coming from Joe's plane. The presumption was that Joe was dead. Then one day, Eloise took a letter from the mail box. It was a letter from Joe saying that he was a prisoner. Later Joe managed to escape, and with the help of partisans made his way back to his base in Italy and finally home.

Sometime after that, we received the news that our country had dropped an atomic bomb on Hiroshima and one on Nagasaki. The war with Japan was over shortly and the Mt. Home community began to receive back its sons and daughters who had gone to war. Folks from everywhere came with them.

Baxter County in the 40's was still "back in the woods", at least, parts of it. The newspaper carried the story of a man out in the county who caught his wife and a neighboring man in a compromising situation. He shot both of them and was put in the county jail in Mt. Home. I felt that I should go to see this man and tell him about Jesus. The sheriff was lenient enough to let me in the cell with the man. How was I to approach the matter? I started with small talk: "How are they treating you in here?" He said, "All right, but I'd rather be home." "Where is home, where do you live?" I asked. "Down there by the river," he said, nodding his head in the direction. "I am sorry you have to be in here," I said. He answered, "Me too, but I had to do what I did." "Do you have a Bible?" I asked, hoping he might open up a bit. "No." He shook his head. Wanting to get to the reason for my visit, I finally blurted out, "Did you ever hear about Jesus?" He thought a moment and then answered, "Seems like I have." But he wasn't sure. I can't remember what happened after that. I was not prepared to talk with a person about giving his life to Jesus when he was not certain he had ever heard of Jesus.

One day word came to the church that a family across the lake was destitute. The church people brought canned food, packaged foods, fresh fruit and vegetables, etc. They sacked it up, and I agreed to deliver it. Bill's brother, Clayborne, was visiting us at the time and volunteered to go with me. We crossed Norfork lake on the ferry and continued along the highway and up a rural road which came to a sudden end. We saw a man in front of a house near the road and asked him how to get to the house of the family to which we wanted to deliver the food. He said, "I can't tell you so you get there, but I will lead you down there. We'll have to walk from here. He can come up here and get the food later."

With that our helpful friend started down the mountain. We followed. After several minutes of following paths, we came into sight of a cabin. Our guide stopped and pointed, "There it is. We'll go on down there." There was a dilapidated fence around the house, and a gate at which we stopped. Our guide called out, "Hello in there." Not a sound came from the house. Although it was winter, no smoke came from the chimney. We waited. Finally, the door of the cabin cracked open a couple of inches and the barrel of a gun appeared. Our guide hollered out, "Old John, come on out here. We don't want your gun; we want you." I turned to our guide quickly and said, "You tell him why we are here." I was afraid the man was making moonshine and might mistake us for revenuers. I wasn't dressed like a preacher, nor was my brother-in-law. After the explanation for our visit, an old man came out of the cabin with a Winchester cradled in his arms. We visited, told him we were from the Methodist Church in Mt. Home and had heard he could use a few groceries. He said that was true and thanked us. Before we left, he hitched a mule to a ground sled and we started back up the mountain to the car. When we had transferred the groceries from our car to his ground sled, the old man said, "Much obliged,"

I remember Carl Keys, entrepreneur extraordinary. Nothing was impossible for Carl. He was a SeaBee at heart. And Mt. Home needed people with dreams and courage. Growth would come to this area, no doubt about that. No one dreamed how much. One day Carl was telling me about the dam that was going to be constructed on the White River at Bull Shoals. I was thinking about the establishment of a Methodist Church in the new town which was to be built. So Carl and I set out to see the area. First, we set out for the dam site itself. We left the road, made our way thru a pasture, opened a gate or two, and finally stood on the ridge overlooking the valley of the White River. There was a marker under our feet. Carl pointed across the valley to a target on the other side and said, "That is where it's going to be. It will stretch all the way across this valley. Do you see all that bottom land up there to your right? All of that land will be covered with water." Not then, but later, I thought about the displacements which that lake would necessitate–the cemeteries that would be moved, the farms inundated, the life-long homes of people torn down, churches moved to higher ground. Wouldn't it have been appropriate for the last song in one of those churches to have been, "Lord, Plant my Feet on Higher Ground"? I thought about the displaced crows who for generations had pulled up the corn growing in the bottoms along the White River. Later I saw them walking the lake shores hoping a bass would run a minnow out on the bank. That was a passage for crows.

Then Carl and I cruised the area to see what construction activity we might spot. Carl was in the lumber business. Driving along, we saw a man clearing off a spot next to the highway. Carl said, "See that? They are going to build something there. Wonder what it is." "Well", I said, "I will ask him." And I did. I didn't linger long after the answer of the ax wielding laborer. When I got back to the car, Carl asked, "What did he say he was building?" I answered, "He said that he was building brush piles."

You may have already guessed why I named this chapter as I did, but I will spell it out. Norfork Dam had been finished as I arrived in Mt. Home. Bull Shoals Dam was about to be completed when I left. Therefore, these experiences took place between two dams.

I have mentioned the church building. Woodpeckers lived in the steeple. They often hammered on the loose siding during worship services. The ushers would slip outside and shew them off. I wanted to end this ritual once and for all, so one day I got out my shotgun and proceeded to decimate the woodpecker population on the steeple. After a volley or so, I heard a shout from below the church in the direction of a tin roofed house of an old German gentleman. Although I could not understand the German, I got the idea that he did not enjoy hearing the pellets fall on his tin roof.

Plans for a new church were soon on the drawing board. The architectural plans presented by John Parks Almand seemed so visionary at the time. But they were woefully inadequate, as time revealed.

It was during this period that I became a Rotarian. At first, the meetings of the club were held in Cotter, a town about eight miles away. But after a year or two, a club was organized in Mt. Home and I became a charter member. I can still see Ray Ramey, Mr. Rotary, in those parts, standing on a chair and leading the singing of "Little Liza Jane". Forty years later I was invited back to the club to give a speech.

I remember Jeff Lunsford, US Engineer, who gave me Ole Zipper, a big, stubborn, male, English setter. I was never able to teach that dog not to jump into a covey of quail. Jeff told me that to train a dog you had to know more than the dog. O well—

I remember a good many other U. S. Engineers. Of course, the old settlers in the area looked at the engineers with a jaundiced eye, but those engineers and the work they did changed the whole course of history for the Mt. Home area. Here I list a few I knew: Lew Park, Lincoln Sherman, Roy House, George Hardin, Pat Patton, Claude Mayo, Jesse Story, all Methodists—and many others who belonged to other churches. They lived in a special village which had been constructed for them by the government.

I remember Tom Shiras, editor of the *Baxter County Bulletin,* but almost at retirement by this time. He was one of the few who realized something of what the dams on the Norfork and White would mean to this area. He editorialized this dream, writing about the "thousands of wild horses stampeding down the valley of the White" just asking to be harnessed and converted into electrical power. That dream came true. I understand that this editorial is printed on the pages of the *Congressional Record* of the United States.

I remember the doctors in the area. Seldon Chambers, Elisha Gray, Ben Saltzman. It may be that Seldon Chambers saved my life when some sort of infection struck me down. Penicillin was just beginning to be used. He and his nurse made trip after trip to my house giving me shots. Elisha Gray made a most significant contribution to this area, one of which was the bringing of Ben Saltzman to Mt. Home. Ben was a Rotarian paradigm, humanitarian, extraordinary physician, and medical leader. He brought our first child, Paul, into the world. Ben's parents were faithful Jews. His mother once asked Ben why he had not settled in a city where he could make more money. His answer was classic: "Mother, when I walk down the street in Mt. Home, people say to me, 'Hi, Ben'".

One Sunday afternoon the Methodists had planned to have a baptismal service on the sandbar where the Buffalo River joins the White River. I don't suppose it is there now, but at that time there was a huge white cross erected on the bluff on the other side of the river from the sandbar. It was a favorite place for baptismal services. That Sunday afternoon, as Bill and I drove to the spot, I noticed more traffic than usual heading in the direction of the river. What I soon learned was that not only had the Methodists planned a baptismal service at this spot, but so had the Baptists, and the Church of Christ, and the Mennonites—and at approximately, the same hour. There must have been 200 people on the sandbar that Sunday. What should be done, who had priority, etc.? Well, the preachers got their heads together. I have since that time referred to this as enforced ecumenicity. We divvied up the parts of the service, one taking a prayer, one leading the singing, etc. The ecumenism of that moment was beginning to impress me. When it came my turn, I led my group of candidates out into the water and baptized them. As we started back to the bank, hand in hand, the people on the sandbar began to sing, "Shall We Gather at the River, the Beautiful, Beautiful river. Gather with the saints at the river. That flows from the throne of God." Almost in tears of joy, I looked back over my shoulder to the cross at the top of the bluff, and the words of another hymn came to mind. I thought, "This could not have happened, except 'Beneath the Cross of Jesus'."

The four and a half years at Mt. Home were wonderful years. I like to think that I grew in my ministerial skills and my personal faith. I was full of vigor, still acting as if my work for the Lord would be my salvation. But I was ready for a change in appointments. As Bill and I rode back from Annual Conference that fall of 1949, having been reappointed to Mt. Home, I said, "Bill, I have a feeling that we'll be moving from Mt. Home before long, and that I will not be pastor of a church." She quizzed me about the kind of work I would be entering. I said, "I do not know, but it won't be the pastorate."

Things rocked along as usual, and then came the announcement that Glen Sanford, the Executive Secretary of the Town and Country Commission of the North Arkansas Conference, was moving to New York to be the head of the national Town and Country movement. As soon as I heard it, I said to Bill, "That's it. They are going to offer me the job that Glen Sanford has vacated." And that is what happened. This may have been the second time that I was a little clairvoyant.

Paul was a toddler. Bill was pregnant. The walls of the new educational building were about five feet high. We bought a new car, Chevrolet—black, and started packing for Conway.

10

On Carrying a Mattress

For a second time, at least, I had experienced precognition. I had told Bill that they would appoint me Secretary of the Town and Country Commission of the North Arkansas Conference. I don't know how I knew this, but I did. They appointed me to this job, headquartered in Conway, Arkansas, with office at Hendrix College. It was in the middle of the conference year, that is, November. The meeting of the Annual Conference had been changed from November to June.

We did not own furniture, since the churches we had served had provided it. This new job did not provide a parsonage and furnishings. The move to Conway meant that we must beg, borrow, buy, (not steal) some places to sit, sleep, cook, eat on, put our stuff in, store our books in; etc,. It meant we must find a place to rent, for buying a house was out of the question.

Mrs. Phernia Morris, treasurer of the church at Mt. Home and wife of the banker, had approached us in the early months of our ministry in Mt. Home and suggested, really told us, that we should be saving some of our salary and that she would hold back $25 a month. We thought this was a bit beyond her responsibilities as a church treasurer, but agreed to it. The five or six hundred dollars she had set aside really came in handy when we faced the necessity of furnishing our new place to live. Moreover, Bill's parents gave us a bedroom suit. A local furniture dealer arranged for us to buy furniture at wholesale from Lyons Wholesale Co. in Little Rock. It all came together without any indebtedness. Mr. Trent of Conway had just completed a duplex which was a few blocks from the Hendrix campus. We rented one side and moved in with our new furniture.

My new job involved much traveling. Fortunately, they provided a station wagon. I think my salary was $4200 a year, plus rent and expenses. It was a promotion from the Mt. Home Charge. I did not like being away from home with Bill pregnant, but everything had worked out so well that I thought I was doing the right thing.

I hit the work road as quickly as I could, not providing as I should for old Zipper, my big, male English setter which Jeff Lunsford had given me. Since there was no fence around the back yard of this duplex, I put him on a long chain—too long, as it turned out. Zipper climbed up the high wire fence which separated our yard from a neighbor's. The snap on his collar somehow snapped on the top wire. Bill Bell, who lived in the other side of our duplex, found Zipper hanging from the wire, took him down, and buried him. I felt guilty that I had not foreseen this possibility. He was a good dog.

My new job as Secretary of the Town and Country Commission was to promote the work of the churches in small towns and the open country. The Methodist Church in Arkansas is made up of small churches, many less than one hundred in membership. Pastoral leadership for these churches in which, by the way, many ministers had heard God's call to preach, was an increasing problem. There was just not enough money available from the churches to pay a decent salary to pastors. As a result, rearrangement of charges was a constant struggle. (A charge is a church or churches under one pastor). A charge with one church is called a "station"; two churches on a charge is a "two point work"; three or more is called a circuit. However, when several churches are served by two or more pastors, they call the arrangement a "larger parish". This was what Byron McSpadden and I developed in Baxter County. It was called the Mt. Home Larger Parish.

So, part of my new job was to work with district superintendents in the arrangement of charges so that pastors would have a decent salary and the churches would have decent leadership. Training schools, revivals, conferences, and meetings with pastors of rural churches were important parts of the work. Anything that concerned the effectiveness of small churches was a part of my job.

Of course, I needed to know what was being done in other parts of Methodism, so I attended a convocation in Chicago Temple Methodist Church. It was the first time I had been to such a large city. I was impressed by this church right in the middle of the loop in down town Chicago. Horizontal space being precious, they built up, not out. The temple was no exception, the tallest Methodist Church in the country, I think. As I sat alone one day in the sanctuary of that great church, thinking about my new work, and about my chosen work as a minister, I felt something not easily explained. As I look back upon it now, I think these were my first misgivings about the way my salvation comes. I had been very hard at work in the Mt. Home Larger Parish, and had enjoyed success. Just maybe I had been depending upon my good work to save me in this world and for the next. But things were different now. I was not getting the "highs" in this new work, the inner satisfaction. I had been taught, and I preached, "salvation by grace". Nevertheless, I began to wonder if I had been practicing what I knew and preached. Could I have been practicing "salvation by works"? As I sat there in the sanctuary, in semi-darkness, looking toward the altar and pulpit, suddenly I saw a cross that I had not seen before. It moved me. I do not understand all that was going on in my mind, and I am sure that what I write now is not entirely factual, but that cross seemed to say that it was the way to my salvation. God gave His Son; the Son gave his life. That grace of God is what saves me, not anything that I do. I thought again of that stanza of "Rock of Ages" which reads, "In my hand no price I bring, simply to the cross I cling."

Glen Sanford, my predecessor, had done a splendid job in rural church work. Surely I could follow his example.

Nevertheless, I didn't—maybe, couldn't. There may be other times in my ministry when I deserved an "F" for failure, but this time on the Town and Country Commission was surely one in which I deserved a big fat "F". I felt frustrated almost from the start. For one thing, the job was so big, the waters so uncharted, that it was overwhelming. I felt, as I moved farther into the job, that the district superintendents were in a far better position to be effective in this work. And, of course, I did not have the authority possessed by the D.S's. Once in a meeting, I expressed some of my feelings about my work. I said, "I feel like a man trying to carry a mattress up some stairs by himself; i.e., I know I could carry it, if I could just get hold of it."

The other reason I was dissatisfied in this new work was that Bill was getting bigger and bigger. One day while I was at a meeting in the home of S.B. Wilford, Batesville district superintendent, I was called to the telephone. It was Bill who had just been to the doctor. Those in the room heard me exclaim, "Twins?" Bro. Wilford had twin teenage boys who heard my cry of utter bewilderment. One said, "Bring him the smelling salt." The other said, "No, bring him the Hadacol." Hadacol, my dear reader, was a popular patent medicine of that day. It might not help your ailment, but it made you feel better, being about 75 percent alcohol.

Bill and I lived uneasily with the news of "twins" for the last three weeks of her pregnancy. Bags were packed and plans were made to take Bill to the Little Rock Baptist hospital at the first indication of labor. That day arrived while I was home (Thank you, Lord). Kathleen Bell, our duplex neighbor and girlhood friend of Bill's, helped me get Bill into the relatively new black Chevy which we had brought with us from Mt. Home. I drove fast. Kathleen and Bill were in the back seat timing the contractions. It looked like the babies would come before we could drive the thirty miles over the old and winding highway 65. I passed cars on the shoulder and exceeded the speed limit, just hoping a policeman would appear to clear the way for me. He didn't, but we arrived safely at Baptist. The doctor had been alerted to our coming and was waiting. They rushed Bill into the room where they took such patients, while I sat anxiously with Kathleen in the waiting room. We had just sat down when a doctor came running thru saying, as he passed us, "We are going to have babies any minute now."

We did. In just twenty minutes, Marc and Chris entered a new world, a month earlier than the normal nine months. They weighed about four pounds each. (Bill can give you the ounces) What would come of these two bundles of possibilities?

For the above reasons, I asked my district superintendent to move me back into the pastorate. I don't think Bishop Martin was very pleased that I had made this decision after only six months, but he agreed. The vocational question now was burning: where will they send me? It soon became known that Bro. Albert Gatlin, who was pastor at First Church, Searcy, was going to take my place. I hoped I would be sent to Searcy. That seemed logical to me. Others saw it differently. During the session of the Annual Conference Saturday night, before they read the appointments Sunday, I ran into Bro. Neil Storey, a district superintendent. Since I had no inkling of where I was to be assigned, I asked him: "Bro. Storey, where on earth are you all going to send me." He replied, "I think we have you down for Tuckerman." I had been in the mountains, now I would be going to the delta.

11

Take this Job and ...

Three boys now. We packed up and moved to Tuckerman, Arkansas. I did not want to go. I had nothing against Tuckerman; I just felt that they had demoted me, and a slight decrease in salary was involved. As I think of it now, I am ashamed that I felt and acted as I did. Someone later asked me if I had ever wanted to leave the ministry. I said "yes", for I was sorely tempted at this time to tell Bishop Martin that "I quit".

I know now that I wasn't seeing things clearly. There are two persons in most ministers of the gospel: one person wants salary raises, larger churches, popularity, acceptance—what the world calls "success". The other person wants to be a humble servant of Jesus Christ like St. Francis of Assisi. For me, and I think for most preachers, there is a real struggle between these two persons. Sometimes one dominates; sometimes, though rarely, the St.Francis in us shows a bit. In the move to Tuckerman, I think I forgot what I had been called to be and do. I wish I had learned my lesson; but, sadly, I was to experience it all again later.

The Tuckerman congregation received us warmly. That always helps. I wish congregations could know how their attitudes support or depress their minister. I know of a young minister who was beginning his work in a small church. Some members were so critical and so uncooperative that the young man left the ministry. In my retirement years, I have spoken to churches about how often they make or break a preacher.

The Rev. Guy Ames, pastor of First United Methodist Church in Newport, a town eight miles from Tuckerman, was of great help to me in my struggle. We fished together and hunted quail together, and he took these times to encourage me to remain in the ministry. Guy Ames was an exceptionally good fisherman and hunter. If you asked him, or even if you didn't ask, he would admit it. But he was not bragging; he could do what he said he could do.

Guy had a jeep with a winch on the front, well equipped for winching the jeep out of the mud which was deep in the" bottoms" where we fished. We were the first fishermen that spring to get into this inaccessible lake. We got into a boat and rigged up with cane poles and live minnows. We caught crappie like nobody's business—slabs, and lots of them.

In the duck season, we went out from Newport into a wooded area where mallards were feeding on acorns in about a foot of water. Four or five of us spread out and walked thu the sparse woods hoping to jump ducks. We saw a large bunch on the water ahead of us. They got up and we shot into them. Our caller went to work and called them right back to us. We shot into them again. We picked up the ducks, our limits, and went home. Great hunting!

One day as we walked along together thru the fields quail hunting, Guy began to dramatize an imaginary meeting of the cabinet which is composed of the bishop and the district superintendents. He would speak for one person and then another. As Bishop Martin, he speaks, "All of you know that Joel Cooper has asked to go back into the pastorate. He has just been in this new job for six months, and now he wants out. Where could we send him?" And then Guy would pretend to be Bro. Storey or another DS: "Who is Joel Cooper. I don't know him. Does he have anything on the ball? Could he serve a church bigger than Mt. Home where he was before he took his present job?" Guy imitates another DS: "Well, I've got a five-point circuit in my district that's open. I'll take him. It will be a cut in salary, but what can he expect, asking to leave a job after just six months?" Guy now assumes the role of Bro. S. B. Wilford, superintendent of the Batesville District. "I'll take him at Tuckerman. Alfred Knox is leaving there." And on and on Bro. Ames would go, until I could finally laugh at myself. That was when I got my head on straight again—for then.

Years later, I held revivals in churches where Bro. Ames was pastor. Still later, I had his funeral in El Dorado.

Although I went to Tuckerman reluctantly, it was one of my best years in the ministry. The members were progressive in their thinking, for the most part. They wanted worship services that were dignified and orderly. A good robed choir and excellent organist enhanced the services. They gave me my first pulpit robe, and I had no problem in wearing it. You must understand that at that time only ministers in large Methodist Churches wore robes. I received persons into the church and we had good attendance. It was one of the best years of my ministry.

It was here that we had our first look at a television screen. It was a snow storm most of the time, but now and then you could see and hear what was happening. We didn't own a TV, but we would go to the Marcus Harris home and watch theirs. I don't think I realized then what an impact this new medium was to have on world culture.

Paul was a toddler. One day he toddled off down the sidewalk toward the church. Bill caught him in about a block. He was getting used to his twin brothers and loved them, I think; but sometimes he pestered them, a habit he practiced until he was almost in his teens. The twins, Marc and Chris, were cute beyond their mother's excited description of them. Bill's parents bought us a twin stroller, a side by side. We rolled the twins almost everywhere we walked. They were sick a lot that winter. Dr. Kimberlin, a devoted member of the church, was our family physician.

The parsonage was an older house, but pleasing. I remember how pleased Bill was with the new electric cook stove the church bought for her. I had learned about hydroponics from Dr. Spessard at Hendrix, so I tried it. I had an old water heater tank split in half the long way, filled one half with sand, set out my plants, watered it daily with the hydroponic mixture. My tomatoes were early, big, and tasty, and I also had a garden in which I raised other vegetables. We needed these, for the $4000 a year salary was just barely enough for five of us.

The church had just completed a building program which included a new sanctuary. To complete the program, the trustees of the church had borrowed about $20,000 from a few of the members. The members had simply signed notes at the bank for various amounts from $500 to $2000. They expected payment in short order, but this had not happened by the time I arrived as pastor. The note holders were getting a bit edgy. Something really needed to be done toward repaying the obligation, so I began to work on it. I went to the note holders with this propositional question: "What will you discount from your note, if I will raise enough money to pay off all the note holders?" This sounded good to the note holders, for they had started to fear they would lose the whole amount of their note. Several note holders promised to discount as much as 50%. I then went to the entire membership and told them the result of my canvas. They responded in a splendid way, and across the year, as the money came in, I would go to the bank and pick up a note. As the year was ending, there was only one $500 note left unpaid. However, I had a $500 pledge from another member of the church. The two people involved were kin. I was afraid that if the pledger knew that his kin was a note holder, there would be no payment, so I kept quiet.

The $500 pledge was not paid by my last day as pastor of the church. I felt a strong obligation to do as I had promised; i.e., pay off all the notes. We had packed our things in the moving van and our boys in the car, ready to go to Conway, my next appointment. I said to Bill, "Dear, I cannot leave without making another effort to collect the pledge and pay off the note." While Bill and the boys waited in the car, I made a call on the pledger, got a $500 check, and went to pick up the note at the bank. The check had been written on another bank and my bank wanted me to get the cash before they would give me the note. Mercy! But I did, and the bank did, and the Coopers left for Conway.

12

Teacher or Preacher

They did not offer me a job teaching at Hendrix, so I really didn't have to decide between teaching and preaching. However, Dr. Matt Ellis, president of Hendrix, told me after our move to Conway that he had decided, if they did not assign me to be his pastor, he would ask me to join his faculty. If they had not appointed me to First UM Church Conway, I would have accepted Dr. Ellis' invitation. That would have turned me toward a teaching career. But, of course, they assigned me to First Church Conway in June of 1951. I think that is what God wanted for me.

I will never know all the "ins and outs" involved in my appointment to one of the great churches of Arkansas. I believe that they appointed me, in part at least, because some ministers did not want to come to Conway First, and some who did were not acceptable by the church. The church had a reputation of expecting a great deal from their pastors. (I have put that as kindly as I can.) Dr. Ira Brumley and Dr. Ellis were most certainly working for me to come to First Church. Just how they worked is the puzzle. I was only 31 years of age, eight years out of seminary. Bishop Martin surely remembered with displeasure my "short" term as Secretary of Town and Country Work. In spite of these blocks, they appointed me.

A month or two before my appointment, I was on the Hendrix campus for something; can't remember what. I met Dr. Brumley coming to the post office. He said quickly, "Joel, go home. You ought not to be around here just now." I knew what he meant. He thought that I might mess up the appointment which was being considered. I went home.

It was very hot in Conway in June of 1951when I rose to preach my first sermon in my new appointment. The church was not air conditioned. When I stood up in the pulpit to preach, I was looking directly into three large exhaust fans in the windows of the east balcony. They helped keep the congregation cool, but the light flickering thru the fans almost blinded me. I suppose the service went tolerably well. I preached a sermon on the greatness of God. That night I preached on "The Joy of Your Religion".

We moved into the "new"parsonage with our three boys. It would never be the same again. The parsonage was built while Dr. C. M. Reves was pastor. The Reves had lived there only a few months, having moved to become the Superintendent of the Conway District. The Stewart family lived in the parsonage for two years. So, it was a NEW parsonage when the Coopers arrived. There were four bedrooms and two baths upstairs, and four rooms and a bath downstairs. Neither Bill nor I had ever lived in such a beautiful and spacious home. There were two sets of stairs in the house. One set led up from the front hall and the other led down into the kitchen. It does not take a great deal of imagination to know how the boys would use these stairs. This parsonage, like the church, was equipped with exhaust fans in the attic. They worked wonderfully.

Before my first sermon at First Church, I did a great deal of thinking and worrying about my abilities and the expectations of the congregation. That's a long way of saying that I was scared. Several of my professors from Hendrix were still active members of the church, including Dr. Ellis, the president, who had been my major professor. Most of the rest of the teachers were members too. Moreover, several teachers from State Teacher's College were members, and, of course, there were the students from both colleges. Add to that what we called the "town and gown" competition, and you begin to see why I approached my preaching task with fear and trembling.

One day I went into the sanctuary, making sure no one was around, and knelt at the communion rail near its north end. I asked God to help me not to fall flat on my face in this new assignment. I don't remember praying, as I should have, for the gifts and graces to be the pastor and preacher that the church needed. I just prayed that God would not let me fail. I am confident now that God did answer my prayer, although it was not a model prayer. At least, I was able to be the pastor for ten years when the average tenure of ministers before they appointed me had been a fraction more than two years.

Dr. Ellis, president of Hendrix, must have thought I had the "makings" of a teacher. One September, the bishop in Kansas called Rev. Ralph Ruhlen, the religion teacher at Hendrix, and told him to come back to Kansas, his home conference, to serve a charge. A shortage of preachers made this necessary. Bro. Ruhlen had met his class once when his bishop called. Dr. Ellis was in a jam. He asked me to teach the New Testament Class. I had no time to prepare and had no experience in teaching at that level, but I agreed. It has been a source of joy for me in later years to meet some students from that class and have the things. Dr. Gladwin Connell, now retired, was one of them.

My beginning salary at Conway First was $5000 a year—no travel, no expense account. That was a lot better than the $4,000 I was receiving at Tuckerman. Still, getting by with our growing family was not easy—Paul, Marc and Chris when we moved, and Clay to arrive before long. The boys would ask to go out to get a dandy dog (hot dog on a stick covered with dough and deep fried). We would sometimes search behind the cushions of the chairs and the sofa to see if we could find the coins necessary for the trip to the Dandy Dog.

However, we managed, for the church raised my salary each year until it was $10,000 at the time we moved in 1961. It was interesting that Joe McGee, reporter for the *Log Cabin Democrat* and member of the Official Board of lst Church, would report in the paper every raise in salary the church gave me. One factor seemed important in considering a raise for the pastor of lst Church: it ought not to get too far out of line with the tenured professors at Hendrix. In those days the salary at Hendrix for a full professor was modest.

The sanctuary of First Church and the educational building were in need of refurbishing. Some members were beginning to feel the need for additional educational space, especially for children. An architect, John Parks Almond, the same man I had used at Mt. Home, was employed by the church to draw up a plan for a children's building to be constructed just north of the sanctuary. The church had to purchase the district parsonage and move it to have enough room for the new building, which would include a chapel, a parlor, and rooms for the children. Also, we had to demolish the old green frame educational building north of the church. It was an ambitious project with an estimated cost of $150,000.

The church employed the Wells Organization to give the church professional help in raising the money for the building program. The company sent Eb Jones to be our fund raiser. He was a great fund raiser, even if he lacked something in his knowledge of English grammar. Someone remarked that he ought to go back to college, but Dr. C.M. Reves, our district superintendent, said, "No, that would ruin a good fund raiser." It was from Eb that I got the saying: "I was so low I could have ridden a bicycle under a rug without making a wrinkle."

I thought the campaign was moving according to schedule, but Eb thought otherwise. He asked me to call a meeting of the Building Committee and the Finance Committee. His speech to the group was very pointed. He said, "I should not take any more of your money for my services, because you are going to fail to make your goal of $150,000. There needs to be at least two big pledges before the campaign has a chance to succeed."

This statement stirred the group. Two of the lay leaders got their heads together and each came up with a $5,000 pledge. Those pledges moved us off high center and the campaign sailed smoothly to a successful conclusion. Afterwards we called this meeting "the night we had the wake". It shocked me to learn from the first day of the campaign that they expected the pastor to pledge one percent of the total. We were tithing already, but somehow we paid what they suggested. Of course, everyone knew the salary I received from the church. It was a part of the fund raising strategy to let the people know what the pastor was pledging.

As a student at Hendrix and a regular attendant at First Church, I had been inspired by the lighted cross on top of its dome. It reminded me of the hymn, "Above the Hills of Time the Cross is Gleaming". When I became pastor, the bulbs in that cross had burned out. Since no one seemed to want to tackle the task of replacing the bulbs, Lamar Davis, associate pastor, and I decided we would take the job. We made our plans carefully. We must wear tennis shoes so that we would not slip as we climbed up the tile roof of the dome. A rope and ladder would be needed. We must fill our pockets with light bulbs. And we must not forget the bug bomb to spray the wasps which were flying around the tupelo. We went into the attic and climbed thru a small window onto the roof. Now we faced the tricky part—climbing up the rounded dome. We made this without mishap, pulling the ladder behind us. When we reached the tupelo which capped the dome, we tied the ladder to it with the rope. I climbed the ladder to the top of the tupelo so that I could reach the panes of glass which enclosed the cross. Having removed a glass side of the cross, I replaced the bulbs. When that was done, we had to retrace our steps, so to speak. All the time Lamar and I were doing this, our wives were watching from the sidewalk across Prince Street, wringing their hands, and praying, I think.

During the refurbishing of the educational building, pigeons somehow made their way thru open windows into the sanctuary. Unable to find their way out, they flew about, perched on the inside rim of the dome, etc. One Sunday morning during worship, I saw a big pigeon sitting on the rim in the dome and looking down at the congregation. I was afraid that at any moment he might come gliding down to circle above the heads of the unwary members. This intolerable situation had to be remedied. Again, Lamar and I took on the task. After considerable thought, we decided to buy some 22 caliber bullets loaded with bird shot and shoot the birds inside the sanctuary. We had to be careful, of course, for the tiny pellets could break the windows in the dome. We aimed carefully and believed that we did no damage to the ceiling while eliminating the pigeons. It was not a pretty sight, but if anyone objects now, let me remind you that the Hebrews sacrificed pigeons on their altars.

Well—

Naom Nechovsky was a refugee from Macedonia who had been interned in a Greek camp, having escaped from a hospital across the lake which separates Macedonia from Greece. First Church people heard of his plight and his desire to come to America. Under the leadership of Mason Mitchell, the church made plans to sponsor Naom and bring him to Conway. Naom arrived, by the grace of God, knowing one word of English—"hamburger". The committee organized to take care of Naom got him settled in an apartment and found a job for him at the Foster Oar Plant.

Often Naom would come to the parsonage to watch television. He liked the commercials because they helped him learn English. Our little boys would watch the television without moving until the commercials came on. Then they would become rowdy until the program began again. This worried Naom, for the reason stated above. One day he tattled on the boys by going into the kitchen and saying to Bill, while pointing to the room where the boys were whooping it up, "It is very. It is very." From that time on our family described any extravagant action by saying, "It is very."

Eventually, Naom was ready to move to Detroit to join a community of Macedonians. After we helped him buy a car and get a driver (he could not drive), he left Conway. He returned later with a young girl and wanted me to marry them. I did not. The girl was underage. He had brought her across a state line, etc. They went to Oklahoma, were married, and returned to Conway before going back to Detroit. We hear from him occasionally. He has found a home in America.

Dr. Aubrey Walton, pastor of First Methodist Church, Little Rock, was elected bishop. Dr. Robert Bearden, pastor of Central Methodist Church, Fayetteville, was appointed to the Little Rock church to succeed Dr. Walton. I hoped I would be appointed to Central Methodist, Fayetteville. I reasoned that I had more experience as a pastor in a college town than any other preacher in the conference and should be appointed. It did not happen. For a second time, the first being Tuckerman, I was depressed.

Again, as I think of it now, I know I had the wrong attitude. I wanted to move up the ladder of appointments and was not thinking of what the Lord wanted me to do or what my real responsibility was. There is no excuse for this attitude, but I had it and had to work thru it again. I did—after sometime. Harold Eggensperger, my district superintendent, was appointed to Fayetteville Central. It was then that I remarked to someone in jest, "I guess I must get on the Conway District before I can ever get appointed to Fayetteville Central." Little did I know then that it would happen just that way.

Clay was born in the old Conway City Hospital, Dr. Keller Lieblong officiating. When this fourth boy became a part of the family, Bill and I gave up having a girl and knew we had enough boys. Clay is probably the only baby born to a pastor and wife while they served 1st Church.

One summer the church decided to have its Sunday evening services in the church yard. It worked well, just a hitch or two. One hitch involved our dog, Reddie, who followed the boys to the outdoor worship service. Since the dog would be a disturbance, I whispered to Paul. "Is this your dog? Take him home." Paul answered, "He's not my dog, but I will take him home." He did—momentarily, that is. The dog beat him back to the service. I asked Marc and Chris, "Is this your dog?" "No", both exclaimed." "Well, take him home anyway." Same story: the dog came back immediately. I turned to Clay, the youngest, "Clay, is this your dog?" Clay answered, "No, but he 'posed to be." This time, I think Clay must have put the dog in the parsonage.

Once, while visiting the hospital, I made a mistake which embarrassed me, but provided a fond memory for another. The church secretary had told me that a lady from the church had a baby by C section. I got the room number from the hospital receptionist and made my way to the room. Thru the open door I could see that the new mother was asleep. I left, but with the intention of visiting her the next day. And did, that is, I tried to visit her. I went to the same room in which I had found the patient the day before and knocked. She invited me in. I did not know the new mother. Furthermore, I realized that I did not know if the baby was a boy or a girl. I thought that the patient was unusually active to have just had a C-section. Feeling my way along, I asked, gingerly, "Tell me, is the youngster a boy or a girl?" The woman looked startled for a moment, burst into laughter and said, "You have me mixed up with someone else. I have just been moved into this room. I understand that the patient before me gave birth to a baby boy. I am—." (She gave her name and rank). She was the maiden dean of women at ASTC.

Years later when I met the dean again, she told me that my visit that day when I asked about the youngster had "made her day" for many days across the years.

When it became known that Dr. Marshall Steel, pastor of Highland Park UMC, Dallas, was to be the new president of Hendrix, a conversation like this took place in the church office:

"Bro. Cooper, how are you going to feel having to preach with Dr. Steel in the congregation?" I couldn't think of a good answer, but while I was trying, a sainted member of the church answered the question. She said, "It won't bother him; he has Jesus Christ in the congregation every Sunday." Touche.

I had a chance to leave Conway before my move to Winfield United Methodist Church in Little Rock. Bishop Martin wanted to send me to Goddard Memorial in Ft. Smith. I did not want to go and, fortunately, the leaders of Conway First were willing to go to see Bishop Martin and to request that I be allowed to stay in Conway. I am sure this did not please Bishop Martin, for when he called me into his office he said, "Joel, you know I can make you go to Goddard." "Yes," I said, "But you cannot make me like to go." The bishop gave in, but it was not a victory for me. I did not have the right attitude. I was still ambitious. I was afraid that going to Goddard would spoil my chances of going to First Church, Ft. Smith sometime in the future. Would I ever learn? Would I ever have the right attitude? At the time, I did not see this sin of pride in which I indulged.

Counseling was a part of my responsibility as a minister that I did not enjoy. However, I had some interesting experiences. One day a man came into my office in Conway and said, "God has told me to kill a man." As I had been taught, I tried to appear "calm and collected" and said, "Tell me about it." He told me that while he had been in the military, his wife had been unfaithful to him with three different men, that two of these had been killed in battle, and that God was telling him to kill the third man. He did not give me the names. I do not remember what I said to him in trying to persuade him that God was not telling him any such thing and that he must not do this terrible thing. He went his way and I never heard from him again, nor do I know if he ever carried out his threat.

When they announced that we would be leaving Conway, Dr. Silas Snow, president of ASTC, invited the Coopers to a farewell picnic in the backyard of the president's home. Sometime during this picnic, Dr. Snow began a conversation with Clay, now about eight years of age, "Clay, I know that your mother and father must move where he is sent, but you don't need to go. Why don't you just stay here with us?" Clay quickly answered, "Oh, no, Dr. Snow, my mother wouldn't take a million dollars for me." This story was told in the Snow family for many years. When Mrs. Snow died, the family told it to me. I was honored to bring the messages at the funerals of both doctor and Mrs. Snow.

About 1960 I attended a lecture in First Methodist Church, Little Rock. When Bill and I arrived at the door of the church, we could see people carrying signs, marching back and forth in front of the church. They were protesting the appearance of the speaker for the day, the chairperson of the National Council of Churches, who had made himself unpopular with segregationists. We were on the alert, to put it mildly. They ushered us down to a pew close to the front of the sanctuary. The service was just underway when an usher came down the isle, went up onto the rostrum, and whispered something in the ear of Dr. Aubrey Walton, pastor. He said something to the usher who then returned to his place in the foyer of the church. The service moved along until the usher came a second time and whispered something to the pastor. Being close to the front, I could see everything but could not hear what they were saying. At this point, I was alarmed, for I was thinking of the pickets outside the church. Dr. Walton, on getting the second message from the usher, consulted with Bishop Paul Martin who sat next to him. They seemed to agree on something, and Dr. Walton stood up behind the pulpit and said: "We have just been told that a bomb has been planted in this church. We think it is a hoax meant to disrupt this service, and we have decided to go on with the program. However, to be fair to you—if you do not want to remain, feel free to leave." One or two persons in the balcony got up and left, plants, I think, but the rest of us stayed in our seats. I confess that I had an almost overwhelming urge to reach under the pew where I sat to feel for a bomb. At that moment, Bishop Martin, without waiting for the organ, started a hymn, "My Faith Looks Up to Thee". I shall never forget this moment when the flow of adrenalin into my veins brought a warm glow all over my body. I think it was caused by a mingling of fear with a sense of pride in standing for what I believed.

It was not all work at Conway. I played some—quail hunting with Bill Montgomery, duck hunting with Bill Farris and Earl Rogers, fishing with Lodie Biggs and W.D. Cole, to name just a few of the church members with whom I played. One spring Wednesday afternoon Bill Farris and I were fly fishing for bream on Lake Conway. Bill knew, although Bro. Guise did the service, that I always attended prayer meeting on Wednesday night. He glanced at his watch from time to time. The bream started hitting almost every time we made a cast. We were having great fun. Finally, Bill said, "We must quit and start back to the dock or you will miss prayer meeting." Now, this is how <u>he</u> told the story: "After I reminded Joel that we had to leave the lake, if he expected to make it to prayer meeting, Joel said, (this is Bill's standard version) The Lord never expected men to go to prayer meeting when the fish were biting like this." I neither affirm nor deny this story.

Once when duck hunting with Earl Rogers, I was short on luck. I couldn't hit a duck, if it had been on the end of the boat. Earl turned after I had missed again and said, "You are a damn good preacher, but not much of a duck hunter." And he was right—at least, about the hunting.

The last Sunday I would be pastor of Conway First was fast approaching. What would I say to the people after ten years as their preacher? I might reminisce, but that might seem to be boasting for some and unwarranted sentimentalism for others. I might "let them have it", "tell them off", "lower the boom". But I didn't really believe I should do this and run to another appointment, unwilling to live with what I had said. I might try to give advice. After all, ten years is a good long pastorate. But I didn't really feel like doing that, even if I had the wisdom. Finally, I decided that I would explain my moving and tell them of my dreams for the future of the church.

Here follows some things I said in my last sermon to Conway First Church, June, 1961.

"My leaving this pulpit may not matter much; but, the leaving of the Coopers is going to hurt the Scouts and the Little League.

"After much thought I have concluded that I have contributed what I am able to contribute to you. I put myself in the hands of the bishop and asked him to send me wherever he wanted me to go. I take consolation in the thought that every Methodist preacher who will behave himself is guaranteed a job somewhere, although "where" is often the question. I want you to know that I do not leave this church because of unhappiness. These have been the happiest days of our lives. You have made them so. You have given me better cooperation than any minister has a right to expect from his people. You seemed determined to give me every chance to succeed as your pastor. If I have succeeded in some measure, the credit is yours.

"You have made us happy by the warmth of your concern for us as a parsonage family. More times than I could ever enumerate, individuals and families have gone to extraordinary trouble to shower us with acts of kindness. Most of these we have not been able to repay in kind; it is impossible. We can only hope that we have been able to make some contribution to your lives in return. We leave you loving you."

"I want to ask your forgiveness for the times I have failed you. Many times I have not been aware of the failure. Blame this on my lack of alertness, my insensitivity to your need—but forgive me. Often I have been aware of failing you. Sometimes I didn't know what to do to help; sometimes I didn't have the courage to try to help; sometimes, sadly, I didn't care enough. I pray your forgiveness for the times I have failed you."

"Now I want to say some things about the future of the Methodist Church in this community. I believe that the next ten years are going to be better in every way than the last ten. This church is going to grow in membership. The gain we had this past year will continue. But the greatest growth of Methodism in this community will be thru a third Methodist Church which you will want to initiate in the near future.

"Look at student work. In the next few days, ground will be broken on the Wesley Foundation building at ASTC. Under the leadership of Vernon Anderson, you can look forward to a more effective program for students than we have ever had.

"And I thrill at the thought of the new pipe organ which will be installed. It has been among our dreams for years. You will be blessed as this great organ leads you in singing the magnificent hymns of the church. I expect it will be a "goose-pimpling" experience the first time you sing with the organ, 'A Mighty Fortress is Our God' Incidentally, some of you have forgotten to turn in your organ pledge. I wish you would remember to do that immediately so the new pastor will not have to worry about that."

"I believe in the future of the church in Conway. This church will become increasingly a tower of strength and a bulwark of faith, not only for those of you who make your permanent homes here but for those thousands of young people who come to these colleges to have their eyes opened and their hands fitted for tools. You members of First church, you are privileged to be in the very middle of this important enterprise which will send its influence for good in ever-widening circles until, at last, they wash every shore of the world.

"We will remember you in our prayers as we trust you will remember us. And although a new relationship and some distance will separate us, it is our deepest faith that we are one in Christ. This is the unity that ultimately matters—and has relevance not only to this world but the next."

At the bottom of my typed remarks, I wrote, "Dr. Ellis has asked to speak"

He did. I do not remember what he said, but I assume it was eloquent, as usual, and was probably a kind word for the Cooper family.

Not everything I said about the future of the church has taken place in the 45 years since I spoke them; but, in saying that the church would grow, I was right. It is interesting that my prediction about a third church being organized in Conway did not come true for about 25 years. It was after I retired that Bishop Wilke asked me to take on the job. But that is a story to be told in a later chapter.

I do not want to seem unseemly, but I think I had a rather successful pastorate for the ten years I was in Conway. The church buildings were refurbished and air-conditioned. A new educational building, chapel and parlor were constructed. The finances of the church were significantly improved. Debts were paid in full. Money was raised for a new organ, although the organ was not installed until after I had moved. Approximately 1000 members were received in the ten years. Sunday School average attendance reached 400 plus during the time that Sue Osment, now Jones, was the educational assistant. And, if I have learned to preach at all, I learned while preaching at First Church—to students, to professors, to average town people. I did not leave because I had to leave. I was ready to move because I felt it was time to move on, that the Kingdom would be better served.

13

"Take Your Seat and Sit Down"

After ten very happy years as pastor of lst UMC., Conway, Arkansas, I was ready for a change in churches. Probably some members were also ready. My tenure was the longest in the church's history then. Bishop Kenneth Pope gave me a choice, something infrequently done in the Methodist appointive system. I had to choose between "going on a district" in the Little Rock Conference and being pastor of Winfield Methodist Church in Little Rock. I chose the pastorate. This was June of 1961.

Winfield became the largest Methodist Church in Arkansas in the years following WWII. It had some wonderfully effective ministers, but other factors were working in its favor. The community around the church was one of the few areas in which returning veterans and their families could find housing. The church building was one of the most beautiful, spacious, and modern churches in the state. By the hundreds they joined Winfield. But as new communities developed on the fringes of Little Rock, families began to move out—to North Little Rock, Mabelvale, Pulaski Heights, joining churches nearer home. Moreover, the Afro-American community began to expand into the vacated housing. By the time I was appointed to Winfield Church, it had been losing members for some time, although it was still a very strong church. In my five years there, I did not help that situation much, if any.

Winfield UMC was located at 16th and Louisiana, in an old and established community; but, the movement and anticipated movement of Afro-Americans into the vicinity of the church, combined with the typical southern attitude toward integration, had put fear into the hearts of many members of Winfield, fear that the church would become integrated or entirely black.

Before I arrived in Little Rock, I began to receive letters which told me, in no uncertain terms, that the church intended to stay "white". Of course, the letter writers did not represent all of the members of Winfield, but they represented a significant minority. I have kept some of these letters. I put three of these letters

86

in this writing to help you understand the quality of air which the people of Little Rock breathed even four years after the infamous Central High School debacle.

The following letter is dated: 5-12-61 and the anonymous writer printed the letter, perhaps as an effort to avoid the possibility of identification:

"Dear Rev. Cooper:

Welcome to Winfield and we wish you at least four happy years here and we think it entirely possible. However Winfield like most other churches is upset and is being torn apart by extreme left wing groups that have invaded our churches. In our opinion the National Council of Churches is dominated by out and out communist (if not they sure are first cousins). Also, Aldersgate and Philander Smith College are merely workshops for the teaching of communism (sit-ins, kneel ins–freedom rides, mob violence, etc.) All under the guise of religion. We are not surprised that a negro was elected president of the Ministerial Association. However, our pastor (Dr. Harrison) assured us at the time (about 6 years ago)the association integrated, that it was a gesture of friendship only. If the preachers really believed that–then they are a lot dumber than their members. You can help build our church back up by denouncing the NCC and by ignoring the negro issue.

We are sick and disgusted with all the stupid mess. We are all white members and we intend to remain all white and that includes our pastor.

A Disgusted Member of Winfield

P.S. Oh yes we do have a certain number of hypocrites in our church too, as you will find out."

I am a slow learner, I guess, for on July 7, 1964 (3 years later) I received the following letter:

"Dear Dr. Cooper,

You know it is hard for me to conceive of a minister of the Gospel creating as much dissent and disharmony in a church as you have created in Winfield.

I was led to believe that the Methodist Church was the most democratic church of any denomination. I was also led to believe that a Methodist minister would listen to the recommendations of the majority of his board members. It seems that I have been grossly mistaken in both of these beliefs.

This much I do know, I am not going to attend any church that accepts Negroes as members. If that is un-Christ-like–then in this one respect, I choose to be un-Christlike.

I grant you your right to your belief, but I question your right to try to force your belief on 1500 members of Winfield Church.

If you follow your present policy and Winfield becomes predominantly Negro, I am confident you will be the first one to 'fold his tent and steal silently away.'

I have nothing against you as a man, but I abhor what you are doing to Winfield Church. If, as some of our members seem to think, you are a very ambitious man with four sons to educate and a deep desire to become a bishop, then I wish you Godspeed.

I shall consider myself a visitor whenever I attend Winfield as long as your Policy stands. For I cannot support your present Policy with either my presence or my presents.

You know, we, who call ourselves Christians, have a code of Christian ethics too, which we cannot violate and live in peace with ourselves and our God.

Presently, I'm getting my spiritual food via television. I never knew we had such uplifting and inspiring messages coming over the air waves. So, as I have always believed some good is derived even from evil things."

To the credit of the author of the above letter, it was signed.

But on with the story. The integration issue came to a head in Winfield when a group of Philander Smith College students decided to "integrate" the churches of Little Rock. At this point, what they meant by "integrate" was simply this: see if the "white" churches would let Negroes attend their worship services. Ultimately, it was a part of the movement (not yet finished) to bring Afro-Americans into the main stream of American life, treating them like the citizens which the Constitution declared them to be, and treating them like the brothers and sisters which the Christian faith declared them to be.

On more than one Sunday, I watched the ushers of the church meet the Philander Smith College students as they approached the church doors, telling them that they would not seat them in worship. (From my study I had a clear vision of the church doors).

Another factor made this a most difficult time for me. I had been riding a bicycle with my boys and exerted myself a little too much. While I was getting my breath, I noticed that my heart seemed to be skipping a beat now and then. To say that this disturbed me is an understatement. While the doctors tried to assure me that it was not a serious matter, I could not believe them. For months I feared a heart attack, and was particularly afraid that I would experience the skip-beats while preaching. I do not include this account of my heart problem at this point in my story because I think the stress of the integration crisis had something to do with the "skips". No. It is to say that I had to deal with this problem while I was dealing with the Philander Smith College students who wanted to see if Winfield would "seat" Negroes. Moreover, it was even more difficult to deal with those church members who were determined to keep the students out.

I was so low that "I could have ridden a bicycle under a rug without making a wrinkle." I had no choice but to "keep on keeping on". I wish my attitude had been like that of Admiral Dewey who said, "Damn the torpedoes, full steam ahead," but it was not. I really had to tread fast to keep my head above water. I did not want to split the church. I wanted to work thru the problem. What could I do? The following statement which I made to a called session of the Administrative Board of Winfield Methodist Church in the fall of 1963 gives the answer.

(Beginning of my statement) "Soon after the bishop assigned me as pastor in charge of Winfield Methodist Church more than two and a half years ago, I requested a meeting of the Policy Committee. From what was said at that time, I understood that Winfield had no policy toward Negro visitors. I took this to mean that negroes would be seated, if they should present themselves.

Last spring two Negro boys from Philander Smith College appeared at our doors and asked to be seated. They were not seated. I did not know that these boys were coming and was not advised of their coming until after the morning service.

Since I had believed there was no policy against seating Negroes and since they had not been seated, I requested another meeting of the Policy Committee. At this second meeting I was told that Winfield had in fact had a policy against the seating of Negroes dating back several years. It was then that I expressed openly and (I think) clearly my conviction that such a policy was morally wrong. The Policy Committee arrived at a plan to talk with groups within the church about this matter. Several group meetings were held, involving perhaps forty or fifty persons in all, in which each person present was given an opportunity to express his/her convictions on the matter. At each of these meetings, I stated my convictions again that the refusal to seat Negroes was morally indefensible. Finally, it was felt by the Policy Committee that nothing was being accomplished by the group meetings, and so no more were held.

Nothing more was done about this matter until this fall {c. 1964} when, once again, Negroes asked to be seated and were denied. Again, I did not know that the Negroes were coming. As a matter of record, I was not here on that Sunday. This second attempted visit and the refusal to seat brought the matter to focus again.

It was then that I began to hear from a good many people on both sides of this issue. This ought to be said–there are two sides to this. There are those who think we should have seated visitors a good while ago as well as those who think we shouldn't. I began to hear from both sides. I think all of you can see that this is not an enviable position to find oneself in–a kind of "between a rock and a hard place" position. Letters came, telephone calls came, visitors to my study came– and on both sides of this issue. Each wanted me to do something to support his/ her position. If you don't know what a dilemma is–this is a good example. You just can't sit on both horns of this dilemma.

Again, I requested a meeting of the Policy Committee, but this time I asked the committee to support me in leading our church to seat Negroes. I was not able to get unanimous support. The meeting was adjourned with the understanding that no decision had been reached.

Then came an Official Board meeting when it was rumored ahead of time that the matter was going to be discussed. We had good attendance, but no one brought up the matter until near the close of the meeting when a question was asked about the status of the matter. The chairman answered that the matter was still before the Policy Committee.

Again, the Policy Committee met, and again,I was unable to get unanimous support for seating. The committee was divided equally or almost equally.

In the meantime (back at the ranch) I got in touch with the students who were systematically testing the seating practices of Methodist Churches in Little Rock. Two of them came to my study and we discussed the matter in detail. I also had a number of telephone conversations with them. Because this line of communication was kept open, I have been able since before Christmas to keep them from visiting us. This about brings us up to date. There has been nothing sinister or secret about the work of the Policy Committee or the pastor.

That we must reach a solution to this problem is apparent to all of us. The situation has been in a state of indecision long enough. We needed this period of debate and discussion; it was not a matter to be decided quickly. But now decisive action must be taken. The prior question, however, is the question, who has the disciplinary right to make this decision? After all, it is the Discipline of the church which tells us how The Methodist Church is to be operated. As Methodists we recognize the authority of the Discipline; this is a part of the vow which we took when we said we would be faithful to the Methodist Church. Every organization has to have an authority, else there is anarchy and disorder. That authority in the Methodist Church is the Discipline, a book of laws and regulations formulated by the General Conference which is composed of duly elected representatives from the annual conferences of Methodism.

Now the Discipline puts certain responsibilities upon the pastor in charge. Among these is the responsibility of deciding who can be members of the church. This is an awesome responsibility, but one clearly placed upon the pastor. As to the decision on the seating of Negroes, the Discipline does not mention specifically whose responsibility this is to be, for the clear assumption of the Discipline is that all persons who approach the doors of a Methodist Church will be seated. There is nothing in the Discipline which can be construed to mean that Negroes can be denied seating. Indeed, there is so very much in the Discipline which implies the opposite. Therefore, I must assume that the responsibility placed upon the pastor to see that the Discipline is followed places upon the pastor the responsibility of saying that Negroes shall be seated when they present themselves.

I think you can understand my reluctance to accept such a responsibility. It would be much easier on me if the Discipline said, "Put it to a vote". But this isn't the Discipline. Some matters are subject to vote by the local congregation and their duly elected boards and committees, and some things are not. Now, you may not agree with the Discipline, but as a Methodist it is your responsibility to comply with it. If you desire, you may seek the authorized way of changing it.

What does this mean for us at Winfield? It means that our practice of not seating Negroes is illegal, according to Methodist law. We are outside the law of the Methodist Church when we refuse to seat Negroes. We are taking the law into our own hands, individual by individual. Is this the position we want to be in at Winfield? Even if we disagree with the Discipline, we don't want to be in the position of disobeying it.

Or, look at it this way: the spirit and direction of Methodism is desegregation, just as it is the direction of our society, clearer every day. I doubt if any of you will disagree with this. What I am asking you to do then is to follow your church. If you don't agree with this direction of your church, then seek out the accepted ways of trying to change this direction, but follow your church. Some very fine brains and hearts, your elected representatives and others across Methodism, have worked out the direction and spirit of your church. Don't push this aside as if it had no merit. Follow your church. Have you read its pronouncements, its Social Creed, the resolutions which come from every conference? The direction in which the church is moving is clear.

Already in this city a number of Methodist Churches have seated Negro visitors and with little stir. Among these are Pulaski Heights, First Methodist, Trinity Methodist, Markham Methodist. Some Methodist Churches have not yet had visitors, but have indicated that the visitors would be seated if they come. Among these are: Lakewood Church in North Little Rock, and Oak Forrest in Little Rock. There may be others that I do not know about. Follow your church—that's all I am asking.

Or look a moment at the ministers of The Methodist Church. I know many of them in Arkansas and I know that most of them are moving in the direction I have indicated. It isn't that you drew a freak when I was appointed as your pastor. My convictions here are not unique at all. You could have done worse, believe me. The point is: we believe that we best serve the church when we preach and work for the things we feel to be God's will. This is freedom of the pulpit and acceptance of the pastor's leadership in areas where he is given responsibility. Do you want to give up this concept? Are you prepared to accept the consequences of a church in which the people vote on what the preacher is to preach and take over the responsibilities which the Discipline puts upon the pastor? I don't believe you want this. I think you want a pastor and a preacher who will stand up and say what he feels to be God's will regardless of what you think or anybody else thinks. You don't want a parrot for a preacher or a puppet for a pastor. I don't think you really want us to keep quiet when we think the church is involved in sin. You wouldn't respect us and we wouldn't respect ourselves. Now, this isn't to say that ministers are infallible. (I won't have to argue that point) We make many mistakes, but because of the uniqueness of our calling we have no alternative but to preach and work for that which seems right. And, in this case, with the Discipline and the Council of Bishops, indeed The Methodist Church at large behind us, we have every reason to proceed. My point again: follow your church.

Now, I want to talk about some practical considerations. First, I believe that our practice of not seating Negroes involves us in the completely untenable position of having to be on guard at every worship service from now on. Practically speaking, this is untenable. Our worship is disturbed, our ushers are imposed upon, we run the constant chance of being involved in headlines. Even if we had no moral or legal convictions on this matter, it would be the part of wisdom to seat our visitors without ostentation.

Second, what is involved in this particular case is simple. A small group of Philander Smith students have decided to see if Methodist Churches in Little Rock are willing to practice what they have been preaching all these years. Now, I must admit that it is inconceivable that much worship is involved here. If I were the visitors, I'd be so scared I couldn't worship. What the students are doing is simply seeing if we are willing to put our preaching into practice. You may think this is a wrong motive, but did you ever come to church with a wrong motive? Nobody kept you out because they thought you had a wrong motive. You see, we are not to give or withhold seating on our judgment of motive.

So, these students are systematically visiting the churches of Little Rock. They do not want membership. I have asked them about this. All we are faced with at present is the question of seating a few Negroes now and then. Now, when you say–"but this is going to lead to something else," I would have to admit that it may. I confess quickly that I do not know in advance the answers to all the problems which may arise in the future in this area. I only know that it is morally wrong, Methodistically illegal, and practically untenable to continue our present practices.

Now, I want you to know that I have not attempted to organize board members to support me in this decision which I am making tonight so that by sheer weight of numbers I could impose my decision upon you. I have no way to enforce what I am suggesting and have sought no way. I am only asking as your pastor that each man in his own mind and heart, closeted away from the pressure of what his fellows will think and unmindful of the things he has said in unguarded moments–I am asking that each man here decide anew what he should do under God. Your decisions will be registered by our actions in the days to come. I appeal to you to stay steady and to use your influence to steady others. Take the attitude: "I'll wait and see. My church and I don't agree, but I'll wait and see. I'll not be the first to jump over the traces." There need be no loss in membership of this church. There have been no great losses at Pulaski Heights or First Church. You are as good churchmen as they. I know you are. I believe you will show this churchmanship in this area as you have shown it so excellently in other areas. I believe you can follow this request of your pastor and that our church can get over this hurdle and onto the more important one of evangelism.

After soul-searching and prayer, and by the authority given me by the Discipline, I respectfully request each of you in his own church position to follow the law and spirit of The Methodist Church by seating and accepting the seating of all visitors to our services without regard to color." (End of my statement)

Of course, I did not convince everyone by my presentation to the Board. And that is an understatement. Within a day or so after I gave this statement, I received the following letter:

"Dear Preacher, I am so sorry that what happened at our church Wednesday night did, but it has happened. The water can't be scooped up and returned to its proper place. Not on the Board so have only heard some of the story. But enough to pass judgment. But the men who were there says you are insistent that we have Negroes in our church. This does not suit me. The Sunday they are admitted is the one (Name) will move somewhere else. Also my family is sick and tired of the "Negro" sermons on Sunday. My thinking is same as a good many others. Know it will hurt Winfield financially. So think you should slow up. There isn't any excuse for us to have Negroes–Niggers what not in Winfield when there are three good Negro Methodist Churches in our part of town. As you know it is the members who pay your salary not Bishop Pope. Yours truly,"

And he signed his name.

Some members of Winfield moved their memberships, not many. There was an organized effort to force my hand by withholding pledges to the church budget. Many of the pledge cards came back to the office with these word written on them: "Not pledging at the present time." Several thousand dollars were involved. The Finance Committee just cut the budget back to our expected income and we moved on. It is to the credit of many members who had delayed their pledges that they paid what they had been paying and the church survived.

I say again: this was a very difficult time for me. I cannot tell from my notes just when or under what circumstances or for what purpose I wrote the following, but it was sometime after the statement I made to the Administrative Board. As I read it, I realized that it might be very similar to what I would say to a local church today in light of our division on the homosexual question. I give only snatches of it.

"I go to Annual Conference tomorrow. It is gratifying to know that we have met all our financial obligations in full ... I am not able to report statistical gains in membership, attendance, etc.... This year has been a period of adjustment to changing ideas and practices in the church ... This adjustment has not been easy for you nor for your pastors. Many of you have been pulled between long held social concepts, on the one hand, and loyalty to your church and pastors, on the other. This has been a difficult time for you. But I would like you to know that it has been difficult for your pastors too. For we have been pulled between a deep concern for the convictions of individuals and the unity of this church, on the one hand, and the call of The Methodist Church and what seems to us to be the call of Christ, on the other. To live in this tension is not easy, but is the occupational hazard for Christian ministers today ...

This does not mean that we are all of one mind, but we do not have to be. We can believe different things and all be Methodists. This has been the genius of Methodism–freedom of thought ... However, we are not free to act as we choose and still be good Methodists. The duly elected delegates (lay and clergy) at General Conference chart the course of action of The Methodist Church. They expect us to follow that course ... My appeal to you, then, as we move thru these difficult days of adjustment to new concepts and new practices in the church—is that you think as you must but that you stay loyal to The Methodist Church. If this is done, then The Methodist Church will become increasingly what God wants it to be, and you will be moving along toward God with it."

After I retired, I said that the Winfield appointment was wonderful, but that the timing was wrong. I started my ministry there not too long after the Little Rock school integration crisis. That issue dominated the scene for the entire five years I was privileged to serve this wonderful church. I took my stand where the church stands. If it had not been for our connectional system, the support of great lay persons, my district superintendent, and my bishop, I would have died there–professionally if not physically.

But I had someone at my side every step of the way–my wife Bill. As I think about it now, I know I did not begin to understand the travail thru which she had to go. She was responsible for caring for four boys, keeping up the spirits of a sick husband, and facing the very real danger of bodily harm due to the stand I was taking. She did this with a grace that is almost incredible.

Bishop Pope received letters objecting to the stand I took on the seating of Negroes. He answered their letters and supported me in no uncertain terms. He was more direct in these letters than I would have been. I know this because he sent me copies of the letters he wrote. He told me after my fourth year at Winfield that he could move me, but that if he did the members would think they forced the move. Not wanting this, he asked me to stay another year. I did. It was Bishop Galloway who moved me back to Conway to be the Superintendent of the Conway District.

Having just read Tim Tyson's "Blood Done Sign My Name", I feel that I must say another personal word—a word of clarification and confession. One. Although we in Little Rock had the school integration crisis which warranted national attention, and the churches of Little Rock were is some turmoil over the "pray in" actions of the Philander Smith students, Arkansas did not have the violence (from black or white) that North Carolina suffered.

Two. I do not want anyone to think that I was a courageous "activist" in the civil rights movement. I should have been more active and more courageous, but, I wasn't. My stand was more theoretical, theological, and homiletical than active. I was not on the Selma march. I never carried a banner. I never protested the seating of Afro-Americans in the back of the bus, the balcony of the theater. And although Orville Faubus walked past my church every Sunday on his way from his church to the governor's mansion, I did not once stop him to ask him why he had taken the stand he did. I was one of those liberals who didn't _do_ very much but preach the "brotherhood of man". If everyone had taken the flimsy position I took, very little progress would have been made in race relations.

"Parts of this chapter are printed in a book entitled, CRISIS OF CON-SCIENCE, edited by James Clemons and Kelly Farr, and published by the Butler Center for Arkansas Studies", 2007, Little Rock, AR 72202

14

Slidin' Elder

The parsonage/office for the Conway District was on Hunter Street, Conway, AR 72032. Dr. Matt Ellis lived next door. By this time Dr. Ellis had retired from the presidency of Hendrix but was continuing to teach. Our son, Paul, had graduated from Hall High in Little Rock and had entered Hendrix. He chose to take philosophy under Dr. Ellis who had been my major professor at Hendrix. I had great respect for Dr. Ellis as a teacher, a churchman, and a person. It pleased me that Paul chose to be in his philosophy class.

Paul took a test under Dr. Ellis and was concerned about the outcome. A day or two after the test there was a knock on our front door. When Bill answered, there stood Dr. Ellis with a paper in his hand.

"May I speak with Paul, please?" said Dr. Ellis in a firm voice.

"Yes, of course, won't you come in? Sit down, please," Bill responded.

"I haven't much time. I just want to talk with Paul about his test paper."

Bill excused herself and hurried to Paul's room and whispered, "Paul, Dr. Ellis is here to talk with you about your test paper."

Paul almost fell out of his chair. He jumped to his feet and hurried into the front room. After the usual greetings, Dr. Ellis tapped the folded test paper on his open hand and spoke in a very serious voice, "Paul, I have read your paper carefully, and I see no reason why I shouldn't give you—" He paused for a moment before finishing his sentence. Paul trembled. Dr. Ellis continued: "An "A", he said with emphasis.

That year with Dr. and Mrs. Ellis as neighbors was a very pleasant one.

Bishop Galloway knew he was going to have "openings" in the appointive system and must have had me in mind for one of them. I think it was Mrs. Galloway who said to Bill shortly after my appointment to the Conway District, "Bill, don't fully unpack." She did not elaborate, but Bill knew that our stay on the district would be short.

It was. One year. After moving from the superintendency of the Conway District, the **College of Ecclesiastical Arts and Sciences,** a fun organization set up by Jim Beal and others, bestowed upon me the honorary degree, *Doctor of Brief Superintendency.* I was given a stole made of black cloth, two inches wide, and instructed to wear it in all subsequent annual meetings of The College. The meetings were always held in the greasiest spoon restaurant to be found.

Bill and I had never been abroad, but I had been appointed as a representative to the up-coming World Methodist Conference to be held in London. Our opportunity was at hand.

We learned that the Robert Arbaughs were planning to attend the same London conference, so we got our heads together and made our plans. Our boys needed someone to stay with them during the three weeks we would be gone. Bill's mother, Mrs. Thacker, and my mother, Mrs. McAden, offered to come to our house and stay with the kids. My sister, Nestel, and Bill's sister-in-law, Louise, would also help. The boys were big enough to do most things for themselves, but an adult was needed.

Bill and I heard about a book entitled, "Europe on Five Dollars a Day." That was for us and we nearly made it, but that was 1966. Bob Arbaugh had been to Europe before and was somewhat "street smart". We set up our reservations, unbelievably cheap. We planned to begin our trip about a week before the conference was to begin so that we could take a "side trip". Our plan was to fly to Paris and make all the tourist stops there. The Arbaughs would then fly to London, and Bill and I would make a few stops in Europe.

While in Paris we visited St. Chappel Chapel. It was the most beautiful room I had ever seen. Incidentally, it was there that Bill left her special sweater, one knitted by my sister Nestel. We hurried back when she missed it, but it was gone. I can't help thinking about St. Paul who left his coat somewhere. Do you remember if he ever got it back?

From Paris we flew to Zurich and did the things there that tourists do. Maybe not everything. It was while we were flying from Zurich to Wiesbaden that I saw the Alps for the first time from the air. I thought it was a bank of clouds, and then it dawned on me what I was seeing. Breathtaking! I had seen the Alps from the window of a tour bus driven by a "mad man". He seemed to have no fear as he wheeled the bus around blind corners on the outside of the mountain, never seeming to mind the possibility of another "mad man" driving a bus meeting us. I didn't enjoy seeing the Alps that way. But looking down from an airplane at 10,000 feet was different and seemed to be much safer.

We were met in Wiesbaden by Chaplain and Mrs. Howard Cox who most generously gave us a tour of southern Germany. Howard had been in school with my brother, John, and his wife had come from Danville, Bill's hometown. Howard was stationed with the army in Pirmasens. Although the Coxes had a sick child, they still managed to take us to many interesting places. Our stop at Worms was of special interest to me, for it was the spot where Martin Luther had said to the Emperor in his trial, "Here I Stand, I cannot do otherwise." I had my picture taken beside this statue and later entitled the picture, "Here I stand, I could not find a place to sit down."

We trudged up a mountain to see a medieval castle and I tried to see a sermon in the philosophy involved. These early Germans shared the idea with many peoples that he who holds the high ground holds the country. Yes, a sermon could spring from that.

We tried unsuccessfully to find a relative of Bill's sister-in-law, Louise Thacker, who lived somewhere in Wiesbaden. We did learn that they were "on holiday" in London. The locals were not much help to us when we showed them the address we wanted. The first German man called in a second and the second a third. They chatted and gestured but concluded nothing. So, we finally folded our tents and left the Germans arguing vehemently.

Somewhere on a tour I noticed that there was much pasture land, but I could see no cows. When I asked the driver about this, he said that cows were kept in the barn all year long and the hay was cut and taken to them. He said it was the most profitable way to handle the feeding of cattle. Strange, don't you think?

From Germany we flew to Amsterdam. As for me, it was canals and bicycles. I did a little impromptu fishing in the canals, but never tried the bicycles. Everyone else did. Bicycles seemed to be common property. When you wanted to go somewhere, you got on a bicycle, never mind the owner, and pedaled off. When you reached your destination, you got off the bicycle never expecting to see it again but knowing there would be another nearby. Well, this may not be exactly the truth, but it is to say that there are more bicycles per square inch in Amsterdam than any place in the world, or something like that.

From Amsterdam we flew to London where we met the Arbaughs. One afternoon we took a hurried trip thru the British Museum. However, museums had lost my full attention by this time, having seen several in Paris, Zurich, and Amsterdam. I had become like the lady who said, "I made the British Museum in 30 minutes, but would have made it in 25 if I had not been wearing high heels."

O yes, the conference. It was held in the Methodist Central Hall just across the street from Westminster Cathedral. I remember more about the cathedral than about Methodist Central. I can't remember how many kings and queens had been crowned there, but it was a very exciting place. Walking in the cathedral, it was a little "goose pimpling", to see under your feet the names, Robert Browning, Alfred Lord Tennyson, etc. We attended "evensong" one afternoon and got the feel of high church worship. Great boys' choir.

One relationship which Bill and I developed at the conference was with a Bishop Wunderlick from Germany. He lived in the same hotel and often rode the same bus to the conference. The good bishop had suffered through the saturation bombing carried out by the allies in the latter part of World War II, but he did not seem to carry any baggage of resentment toward Americans. Incidentally, we met him five years later at the next meeting of the World Methodist Conference on the top of a mile high mountain in Denver. Small world.

Sometime during a break in the conference, the Arbaughs and the Coopers rode a train down to Brighton, a city on the channel, to hear a famous preacher whose name slips me. What I remember about this trip is the dinner after the preaching. It was a pretty fancy place, and sitting near our table was a distinguished English gentleman who was taking this "eating out" very seriously. We were having the time of our lives, laughing, talking (too loudly, I am afraid). Our very proper neighbor was obviously bothered by these "ugly Americans". This made the situation even more hilarious. We had more silver and plates at our disposal than we had ever had at a dinner anywhere before—or since. We took the whole thing as a lark.

Returning home that night by train, we found that all the local trains and busses had stopped running for the night. We tried unsuccessfully to hail a taxi. It started to rain. We were two or three miles from our hotel. There was nothing to do but walk. We made it, or else I wouldn't be writing this.

I can't remember much of what happened at the conference. I do know that it gave me a better appreciation of Methodism as a world denomination.

Bob wanted to take us to the follies. I would not go. He led us toward the place, telling us he was taking us somewhere else. When I discovered his playful deceit, I refused to go further, for I was afraid I might meet someone who knew me. Bob and Mabel went by themselves. Afterwards Bob told me he had seen our bishop there. He might have lied.

Bill served as my secretary during the one year I was a district superintendent. E. W. Martin, treasurer of Hendrix College, was a very helpful district treasurer. I did the usual things required of a DS, including the holding of charge conferences in every charge from Belleville to North Little Rock. I tried to preach in every church in the district, so Bill said, but I do not remember this. I did nothing earthshaking while I was a superintendent, influenced no doubt by the feeling that I would not be on the district very long. I believe I did give help to the members of the Mayflower UM church who were planning a new sanctuary.

Of course, I worked in the cabinet helping to make appointments. One day Bishop Galloway asked me to work out a "round" of appointments. It involved a pastor in the Conway District. I worried about it half the night, but I gave the bishop my suggestion the next morning. He accepted it. I thought it was a good "round", but it did not turn out that way. I cannot give more details for I want to protect those involved.

Here follows some thoughts on the Methodist way of placing their pastors: Appointments of pastors to churches are not made in heaven. They contain the faulty judgments of human beings. Nevertheless, I am convinced that this appointive system of matching pastors to churches is the best system going. Since United Methodist churches do not hire their pastors, they cannot fire them. That means the pastor is free to preach the gospel as he/she understands it, as long as the preaching is not contrary to the Discipline, our rule book. Of course, the local church can have a great deal to say about who will serve as their pastor, but in our system the pastor is protected by his district superintendent and bishop from whimsical action by local churches.

In an earlier chapter, I mentioned that I had wanted to be appointed to Central UMC, Fayetteville, when Bob Bearden was moved from Central to 1st UMC Little Rock. That did not happen then. But seven years had passed and I was now superintendent of the Conway District. I had said once that I guess I can never be appointed to Central UMC until I serve the Conway District. That had been the route taken by Dr. Bearden and Dr. Eggensperger before me. And that was the route I would take, "believe it or not". In June of 1967, after only one year as a district superintendent, I was appointed to Central United Methodist Church, Fayetteville, Arkansas.

The boys would have to change schools again. Moreover, I was still having the "skip beats", extra cystolies is the medical term.

Somewhere along the line of life, I began to grow up spiritually. I began to understand that my "works" could not save me. I knew this with my head. I passed my theology classes at Duke Divinity School. I just had a hard time accepting this with my heart. Finally, I began to accept it: I couldn't preach enough sermons, visit enough sick people, counsel enough sinners, go to enough meetings, read enough Bible, pray enough prayers to warrant my personal salvation. Moreover, my sinful pride weighed heavily on the damnation side of things. I didn't "cuss or drink or run around with wild women", but I was full of pride, concern for reputation, thirst for acclaim, and worldly ambition. I was a sinner. Only God's grace could deal with that.

Just before annual conference I attended worship at First United Methodist Church in Conway. The bulletin read that the next hymn was entitled "Rock of Ages". I sang it with renewed conviction: "In my hand no price I bring. Simply to the cross I cling."

15

"Burn, Baby, Burn"

The Cooper family moved to Fayetteville in June of 1967 where I was to be pastor for an unprecedented 13 and a half eventful years. What I had hoped for had come to pass, but I had not prayed for the appointment. It was Bishop Galloway who appointed me to Central United Methodist Church. I hope it was what God wanted.

I could hear a voice as I sat in my study which was just across the hall back of the sanctuary of Central United Methodist Church, Fayetteville, Arkansas. No, it was not the voice of God, but I listened carefully and made out the words: "Burn, baby, burn." I jumped from my chair, raced out into the hall, and carefully opened the side door to the sanctuary. I looked around to my right and up to the high pulpit. There stood a strange young man who on seeing me stopped his oration. He had on a hat with a brim, and a sash which went over the hat and under his chin. He had no audience.

"What can I do for you?" I asked.

"O, I'm just practicing my speech." he answered.

"Where are you planning to give your speech?" I asked softly, not wanting to further disturb the obviously disturbed.

"O, up at the university somewhere," he said with a crooked grin.

My mind was working quickly, if not very effectively.

"Well, when you get through, come into my study back there and let's visit," I said, in what I hoped was a nonthreatening tone.

"Where is your study?"

I pointed. "It's back there. Just go out this way and down the hall. You'll see the pastor sign on my door."

I wish I could remember what was said in my study, or even if he ever came to see me. I would see him later.

It was not the best of times, those days of the seventies in Fayetteville, Arkansas—or wherever there were students across this country. Not all of them, but many students, or flunked out students who lived around universities, were rebelling—against authority (parental, collegial, governmental), against institutions (ecclesiastical, corporate—anything monolithic.) What sparked this? I am not smart enough to answer that. Some rebels talked about being "a free soul". Where that originated, I do not know, but it translated often into a noncompliance with the status quo and sometimes into violent actions of outright rebellion and destruction. The Vietnamese War was part of the problem.

Of course, all was not right with our society in those days. Brave souls were needed to speak up against the prejudices, the injustices, the miseries, the stupidities of the times. Maybe that is what the "hippies" were trying to do in such clumsy and brainless ways. However, I don't remember that they cried out against these failings of the times. In the words of that young man standing in the pulpit, they said, "Burn, baby, burn."

I was awakened by some noise outside our bedroom window which faced the back of Central United Methodist Church. On going to the window, I peeked out, saw the flashing lights of a fire truck, and realized that something was wrong. I dressed quickly and rushed out to find that the church was on fire. The firemen were hosing down the slate roof of the church. I could not see much fire, but there was smoke, (and you know the rest of that line). Someone explained to me that the fire had started inside the church in the altar area, had burned up the walls into the area between the ceiling and the roof. The roof deck was made of four inch thick planks. It was this deck that was on fire. The problem for the fire fighters was difficult: how do we get water onto the fire which is burning between the slate roof and the plastered ceiling of the sanctuary? As it turned out, the firefighters were not able to control the blaze very effectively and the burning continued for six hours or so. It was arson. Hymn books had been placed on the floor and leaned up against the wall. We never learned the purpose of this action, but it told us clearly that the fire was no accident.

I was standing in the parking lot, 3:00 A.M., Sunday, watching the smoke rise from the burning church. As I look back at that moment, I know I had multiple emotions coursing thru my addled brain—fear, anger, grief, guilt, disbelief. Nevertheless, it was happening—one of the most beautiful sanctuaries in the state was being destroyed right before my eyes. Beside me stood a friend and church member, Curtis Shipley. He was suffering too, for his life was tied into that church.

He shook his fist and said thru gritted teeth, "We'll build it back better than it was."

Finally, I began to think clearly. Where would we hold the morning worship services? Why not Mt. Sequoyah, the Jurisdictional Assembly? I called the mountain, explained our situation, and received permission to hold our morning worship in the tabernacle on the mountain. Next, I called the radio station over which the Sunday morning worship service was regularly broadcast. The manager said they could have everything ready for the service to be broadcast from the mountain. Moreover, they agreed to keep announcing where our service would be held.

The attendance in the tabernacle was good, considering. We began the service and moved to the Apostles' creed. A lump came into my throat as I began the introduction—"Where the SPIRIT OF THE LORD is, there is the one true church, apostolic and universal, etc." I explained what everyone there wanted to hear. "The church is not a perishable building, It is where the Spirit of the Lord dwells in the hearts of people."

I thought I had taken care of everything in making the move to the mountain. But when I had finished the sermon and had given my usual invitation for people to unite with the church on profession of faith or transfer of membership, a lady came forward. She gave her name and said that she wanted to be baptized. It was then that I remembered what I had forgotten. Water. I had no water to use in baptism. Looking toward the front pew, I motioned to a church secretary, Florence Stewart, to come to me. I whispered.

"Florence, please find some water and bring it quickly." She was "out of there". Before the hymn was finished, she returned with the water and I baptized the lady. She had the dubious honor of being baptized out of a Dixie Cup. If, dear lady, you should be reading this, please contact me.

It took a year and a million dollars (insurance covered, thank you, Lord) to complete the reconstruction of the sanctuary. The roof and the interior of the sanctuary were destroyed by fire or by the water used in fighting the fire. Of course, the organ was destroyed. During the reconstruction, we held our worship services in our Fellowship Hall. Our attendance suffered, especially in the summer. The hall was not air-conditioned.

I preached in a short sleeve white shirt without a tie. One Sunday I was to baptize a baby. I took the baby, cradling him in my left arm. The baby burped and filled my shirt pocket with curdled milk and orange juice. The bottom seam of my pocket held—momentarily.

Finally, we moved back into our new sanctuary. O, how we rejoiced, but not for long. After a year of uninterrupted worship, I returned to the church one late afternoon to find the fire trucks all around the church. My instant reaction, "No, God, not again!" Nevertheless, it was. However, this time the fire was caught early and the damage was about $85,000, as I remember it. The culprits had pushed the pew cushions up against the doors and into the altar carving of the Last Supper, and set them afire. The burning rubber had blackened the interior of the sanctuary.

One Sunday morning I was frightened. All across the land in university settings, Afro-Americans had been interrupting worship services in predominantly white churches by demanding reparations for what the white race had done to the black race. The bishop and I had visited some about what ought to be done when this happened at Central. One Sunday morning I was sitting in my chair near the pulpit looking at the people as the ushers did their work. What I saw, caused goose pimples to rise on my arms. An usher was leading a group of Afro-American men down the isle to a seat near the front. The men wore shiny black suits with white shirts and yellow ties—all alike and all very neat and cool. I said to myself, "Old boy, your turn has come." But it hadn't. The men were members of a black fraternity and had just decided to come to Central that Sunday.

One day when I was near the altar in the sanctuary, I saw an envelop tucked under the edge of a candle stick. It was addressed to God. I felt a little strange reading God's mail, but I opened the envelop and read the cry for help from some university girl who had lost her love. I may have kept her letter, but I cannot find it now. She poured out her heart to God and had placed the letter on God's altar, a logical place for a mail drop. I decided that I would try to answer in a sermon the questions she had raised. So, on the next Sunday I told the congregation about the letter and tried to deal with the young lady's problem. As it turned out, the young lady was in the congregation and wrote me another letter. I never knew her name or saw her to know her. She just disappeared into the many university students who came in and out of Central.

Bill and I were sitting one evening at our kitchen table, in the parsonage which was next to the church, when there came a knock at our back door. On opening the door, I saw a young lady in a fur coat. I invited her into our kitchen, and she sat with us while telling her bazaar story.

"I quarreled with my husband and decided that I would end it all. I thought about drowning myself. While he was out of the house, I put on a bathing suit." She opened her fur coat to illustrate her point. Sure enough, she was wearing nothing under the coat except the bathing suit. She continued, "I drove to the river bridge with the intention of jumping. I laid my coat aside, but when I looked down at the water I lost my nerve and chickened out. And now I don't know what to do!"

We talked. Finally, she gave us her home telephone number and permission to call her husband. He agreed that she should come home. She left the way she had come with a "thank you", and disappeared from our lives.

Not long after I arrived in Fayetteville I received a phone call one night. The voice said, "I am an alcoholic and I need your help".

I knew, I think, that alcoholics pick out new pastors in the community, the old ones having lost patience with them. He continued, "Will you meet me in the Springdale Methodist Church to pray for me? The sanctuary is open." It was midnight, and an alcoholic stranger was asking me to meet him in a place five or six miles away, with no one around. I do not know why I agreed, stupidity I guess. "Yes," I said. "It will take me a little while to get there."

I drove to Springdale; found the church; entered the front door, encountered a man who said, "Come, go with me down to the communion rail." I followed the weaving man. We knelt side by side at the rail and prayed. And that was that. I never heard from him again. Do not think this was a saintly act. As I view it now, my action was not wise and was probably pride motivated. It was a part of my recurring attempt to "save myself" by being a "do gooder".

Victor Nixon, who had just graduated from Perkins School of Theology, was appointed as the associate pastor. He served with me at Central for five years. After leaving Central, Victor quickly climbed the ecclesiastical ladder to be a long time pastor of Pulaski Heights UMC, Little Rock, one of the leading churches in Arkansas. Freddie Nixon, Vic's wife, was a soloist and choir member, adding significantly to Vic's ministry. Their daughter, Aubry Kay, is like a grandchild. Bill and I proudly watched her grow into a gracious young woman.

Vic is an effective minister of the gospel, a splendid T.V. pastor. He has the distinction of having read the marriage ceremony for Bill and Hilliary Clinton. The Nixon family is like kin folks. So, I can relate this amusing incident.

I had gone to some meeting out of town and Victor was to preach the sermon for the morning worship. He had a great idea, although I do not know what it was. After preaching a while, he asked the congregation to file out of the church thru one door and return by another door to hear the "rest of the story." Did he ask the people to sing, "We're Marching to Zion", or "Onward, Christian Soldiers"? I do not know. The problem: a good many of the saints did not return to the sanctuary as Vic had planned, thinking they had been given a head start in beating the Baptists to the restaurants.

One day a pretty brunette co-ed from the university came into the office where Vic and I were visiting and said: "I would like to do something for Central". We were excited to have someone so attractive to volunteer to help. I have kidded Vic and Phyllis Hall that Vic turned hand springs right there in the hallway. Phyllis later became a most valued and effective member of the staff of Central.

Paul Schultz, choir director extraordinary, lifted our music program to unprecedented heights. Ken Davis began his music career as director of our youth and childrens' choirs, doing splendid work. Viola Jackman was the Church Secretary, Mary Cotterman, church treasurer, and Jerry Bond, hostess. During those early years we had more different janitors on staff than you can "shake a stick at." However, Jake stands out. Moses may have "leaned on his staff and died," but I leaned on that wonderful staff and lived. Other splendid Associates were: Ron Clark, Bob Clanton, Bob Cantrell, Marvest Lawson, and Kurt Wulfkeuhler.

I officiated at many weddings during my thirteen years at Central. Jerry Bond, our hostess, was a devoted Baptist. One day while preparing for a wedding reception, she saw some young men "spike" the punch she had prepared. When they left, she poured the punch down the sink drain and prepared again her usual non-alcoholic punch. I have often wondered what the young men thought when they tasted the punch at the reception. I can just hear one say, "Gosh, I guess we didn't put enough in it. Too late now."

It was during my pastorate at Central that I was first elected to General Conference. The conference was held in Dallas, Texas, in 1968 and became known as the Uniting Conference because it brought together two denominations: The Methodist Church and The United Brethren Church. In 1968 we were a denomination of about nine million members. Dr. A. W. Martin, retired great leader of the N. Arkansas Conference, accompanied me to Dallas and interpreted for me the "goings on". He had been a delegate to General Conference several times. He was that same district superintendent who left me, as a boy preacher, to finish the revival at Cache Lake. Later, his wife asked me to bring the message at his funeral.

Sometime in the years following my first General Conference, my name was bandied about as a possible candidate for the episcopacy. I put it that way because it is just tacky to say that I ran for that office. This does not mean that I did nothing to affect the course of events. Of course, I tried to put my best foot forward in the best places for influencing delegates. Some would call that "running," I suppose. The delegates gave me significant votes in the Jurisdictional Conferences of 1976 and 1980. You may look back to the first chapter for further details. In any event, I was a delegate to the General and Jurisdictional Conferences of 1968,

1970 (extra conference), 1972, 1976, 1980, all during my pastorate at Central Fayetteville. I do not think I made much of a contribution to the work of these conferences, for I never made a motion or a speech on the floor. Some who did, shouldn't have.

It was time to move from Central. I had been the pastor for thirteen years and two months. I knew it, and some members knew it. George Ivy retired from First UMC, Ft. Smith and Bishop Kenneth Hicks appointed me to be the pastor there beginning September 1st. My vacation started August 1, 1980, so my last Sunday to preach for Central was July 27.

I gave a great deal of thought to what I would say in this last sermon. It would not be a regular sermon with a text, introduction, three points, and a conclusion. It had to cover many bases. While I was prepared, had the sermon written out, I was still trembling. I looked for Bill, and, as always, drew from her the encouragement I needed. The lights were dimmed a bit. The choir director, the organist, and the ushers took their seats. Honestly, it seemed to me that it was quieter than usual in the sanctuary as I began to speak:

"It would have been easier on me, perhaps easier on some of you, if I preached a regular sermon this morning, three points and all, leaving unsaid the things I have in my heart. Nevertheless, 'the time has come, the walrus said, to speak of many things—of shoes and ships and sealing wax, of cabbages and kings. And why the sea is boiling hot. And whether pigs have wings or not'." As I go along, I'll try to say which category I am discussing.

First, I want to say something about my feelings on not being elected to the episcopacy. I was disappointed, of course. I wanted to have this opportunity of serving the church in that arena. But it did not happen and I am in the process of accepting this. I had never prayed that I would be elected. Of course. I prayed that I might be led into that place of service where I could be most effective for the church and kingdom. Now, I do not say, "Well, it wasn't God's will for me to be elected." I still do not know whether it was or wasn't, may never know. What I do know is: it is God's will for me to accept what has happened, to learn what I can from it, and to move on with my ministry, unhindered by the malaise of disappointment. With God's help, I am attempting that. And I ask for your supportive prayers.

Now, a word to you who have shared in my disappointment. Do not linger long in the land of lambasting. It is natural for all of us to look for someone or something to blame for those things which happen to us. I don't suppose mortals can avoid some of this. What I am saying is: don't take up residence in the house of blame. Don't continue long to blame the system, or politics, or this section of the jurisdiction or that. While I am grateful far beyond my ability to express it for the love and support I have had and have from you, I do not want you to spend much more energy thinking about the reasons I was not elected. Someone had to be disappointed. Perhaps I am the appropriate one, having had more practice than some.

Thank you for all your words of encouragement, for your prayers of support, your financial contributions—everything you did to help. I had a fine opportunity to be elected, and I am grateful for that. The men who were elected are strong and good. The church is in good hands. Pray with me that God's strength and guidance might be theirs in the years to come.

So much for losing. Now let us look at leaving. By now you know that this is my last pulpit appearance at Central as your pastor. I was tempted to reminisce, and I will for a few minutes. These thirteen years and two months have been a tremendous personal experience for the Cooper family. Three of our boys graduated from high school here. Two of our boys received Master's degrees from the university. Two other boys were licensed to preach from this church. One boy graduated from the university. One boy married a member of this church and two boys are members of this church with their families. Four grandchildren have been given to us during this period. Fayetteville Central Church is home to our boys.

Bill and I have developed friendships which will last across the rest of our lives. Our leaving will involve us in a true grief experience, for these have been wonderful years, rich and full to the brim.

But more. These years have been very rewarding to me as a preacher. This church has been a challenge from the first day to this day. What an opportunity! I have preached to thousands of different students who attended Central while attending the university. And I have preached to the most responsive membership any pastor could desire. This is a free and great pulpit, very challenging. It has been a distinct honor to occupy it across these 684 Sundays, give or take a few. This does not mean that I think I have met the challenge adequately, but I can say in all honesty that I have tried to preach a balanced gospel which was intended to avoid the excesses of individualism and emotionalism, on the one hand, and the pitfalls of secular humanism on the other.

My pastoral experiences have been rewarding. I have baptized your babies, almost 300 of them, confirmed your youth, received 41% of you into the church, 850 of our 2050 members, married some of you and your sons and daughters, buried your dead, 186 of these, walked with you in crises of illness, brokeness and old age. My heart has been broken and is broken now by the sorrows you have had. Of course, this does not mean that I have been a perfect pastor. I am conscious that I have not been an effective pastor for everyone, but, if I know my heart, I have wanted to be.

My administrative experiences have gone from the sublime to the ridiculous. I have been privileged to lead the church in programs that have been very successful, and I have been awakened from sleep at three o'clock in the morning by a malfunctioning security system. I have worked with a great staff, effective and loyal. And the volunteer lay leaders of this church are unexcelled. I wish it were possible to show statistical gains across these thirteen years, but it isn't possible—may not have been possible, given the climate of most of these years. We have been passing thru the most difficult years the church has known in this country's history. The United Methodist Church has lost 1 million members in this period. Our membership at Central is slightly higher than it was when I came, but worship attendance and Sunday School attendance have decreased about like the national average. We are now raising and spending about twice as much money as we were when I came, thirteen years ago.

O yes, the fires. What a devastating experience! They had a very detrimental effect on worship attendance and the number received into membership. But it was not all bad. That Sunday morning as we sat in the tabernacle on Mt. Sequoyah, we learned the meaning of those words which introduce the creed, "Where the spirit of the Lord is, there is the one true church apostolic and universal." And while attendance was hurt, primarily among the students, I think, you members of this church gave your money as you had not given it before. And we built back without indebtedness on the rebuilding. Enough of reminiscing.

Some ministers in their last sermon before leaving are tempted to "tell them off". I don't have any temptation at this point. You have been so good, so cooperative. I have no inclination but to tell you how much I appreciate you and love you and will miss you.

Now, I need to say a word about the circumstances surrounding my leaving. I can assure you they were as confusing to me as they were to you. I asked the bishop and district superintendent to appoint me to another place of ministry. The Pastor-Parish Relations Committee of Central was kind enough to vote for my return to Central, if I should not be elected bishop. I am grateful for this. But I choose to leave now. The time is right. I have made my maximum contribution to you. I have preached everything I know and a lot I didn't know. I need a new opportunity and a new challenge. And you need a new pastor. With him will come new enthusiasm, excitement, challenge, opportunity. Some of you who have lost interest in the church will have the chance to begin again with new dedication. I pray God you will. So, let it be clear. I have asked to move because I honestly believe it is time.

I hope and I believe that my leaving in this way will make a positive contribution to the work which you do under your new leadership. You will not be unhappy with the bishop or the district superintendent or your Pastor Relations Committee for moving your pastor, because I go by choice. And since I am not unhappy with you as I go, there will be no seeds of dissension left in the church. The new pastor will not find a divided church, part of your remembering how I did it and not wanting to change, and part of you on the other side. No, the new pastor will find all of you ready to cooperate fully as he leads you to achievements for God that I've never dreamed of.

Of course, I am not saying that I want you to forget us. We are human enough to want to be remembered, as we'll always remember you. But I am saying you will be flexible enough to accept new and different leadership and to accept it graciously, prayerfully, cooperatively, and enthusiastically.

Now, to get the whole matter as right as it can be made, I want to ask your forgiveness for the times I have failed you. Many times I have not been aware of the failure. Blame this on my lack of alertness, my insensitivity to your needs, but forgive me. Many times I have been aware of failing you. Sometimes I didn't know what to do to help. Sometimes I didn't have the courage to try to help. Sometimes, alas, I didn't care enough. I pray your forgiveness for the times I have failed you.

Now, I want to say some things about the future of Central. I believe that the next thirteen years are going to be better in every way than the last thirteen.

Take the matter of membership. This church is going to grow in membership. The gain we had this past year will continue in 1980 and beyond. We have grown the first six months of this year.

Take the matter of church attendance. Already this year the attendance has been considerably better than the same period last year. This will continue. The attitude of university students is no longer anti-institutional. Already students are coming to Central in increasing numbers. I expect this trend to continue.

Take the matter of Sunday School attendance. We have made more improvement in this area than in any other area in the last six months. The increased enrollment of young adults and their infants is one of the most promising things happening in the church. Sunday School attendance is going on up.

Take the matter of finances. We are doing a good job. You will not want to slack off during the month of August. You will want to see that your pledges are paid to date, so that the new minister does not have to worry about finances as he comes. If you want to do something for me as a going away present, just keep your pledges paid up to date during August. That will save my face and promote the kingdom at the same time.

Before too long, the chapel will be finished and work can be started on the next project, the kitchen. It is my hope that you will continue one project after the other until fellowship hall and the second floor of Wesley have been air-conditioned and completely revamped. That will give you a very comfortable and adequate plant for the growth you will have.

So, you see, I believe in the future of this church. This church will become increasingly a tower of strength and a bulwark of faith, not only for those of you who make your permanent homes here but for those thousands of young people who come to the university to have their eyes opened and their hands fitted for tools. This church, for United Methodist students, at least, will have as its function the widening of horizons and hearts. You are privileged to be in the very middle of this important enterprise which will send its influence for good in every widening circles until at last they wash every shore of the world.

This is not an ordinary church, not ordinary in any way, but particularly, not ordinary in its opportunity to strike Christian blows where they can do the most good. Be proud you are here with such marvelous opportunities to do God's work.

Another reason why I believe in the future of Central is because of the man who is coming to be your pastor. He is Merle Johnson, presently pastor of 1st UMC Forrest City. Before that he was pastor at Siloam Springs. He is a vigorous leader, an excellent preacher, an understanding pastor and counselor, a writer, an authority on United Methodist beliefs and polity. You are fortunate to be receiving him; he is fortunate to be coming here. Look forward to great days ahead.

Now, this last thing is hard to say, but I must say it for the sake of the church and your new pastor. Let him be your pastor. Let him into your hearts from the day he comes. Let him marry your sons and daughters, let him bury your dead, let him baptize your babies and confirm your youth. I have been privileged to be your pastor. After August 31, I will not be your pastor and I will not expect to exercise pastoral care in the ways just listed. I'll have a new congregation to which I intend to give my best. This does not mean that suddenly I do not care for you. No, I'll always love this church and all of you, but I must ask that you not ask me to return for pastoral duties. Let your new pastor be your pastor.

Bill and I will remember you in our prayers as we trust you will remember us. And although a new relationship and some distance will separate us, it is our deepest faith that we are one in Christ. This is the unity that ultimately matters—and has relevance not only to this world but the next. We'll be on vacation during the month of August and will report to First United Methodist Church, Ft. Smith on Sept. lst.

What I have said today, and for these thirteen years, I have said in the name of the Father and the Son and the Holy Spirit. Amen.'

I gave my usual invitation for people to unite with the church on profession of faith or transfer. At the time for the benediction, I began: "Will you please keep your heads up and your eyes open." As I did every Sunday, I started walking up the middle aisle, turning to my left and right, saying, "May the Lord bless you and keep you. May the Lord cause his face to shine upon you and be gracious unto you. May the Lord lift up his countenance upon you and give you peace—in your coming in and your going out, in your lying down and your rising up, in your labor and your leisure, in your laughter and your tears, until you come to that day in which there is no darkness and to which there is no end. Let God's people say 'amen'".

The choir began, "God be with you 'til we meet again. By his counsels guide, uphold you, with his sheep securely fold you …" I never cry, but the lump in my throat was nearly choking me. I was leaving a church I dearly loved.

16

"A Mighty Fortress"

I parked my car on the street beside the north entrance of the educational building of First United Methodist Church, Ft. Smith. For many years I had wanted to be pastor of this church, although it had come to pass late in my ministry. I had only four years to retirement. The church was a massive structure stretching from one block to the next, a mighty fortress to withstand the "fiery darts of the wicked."

I grabbed a box of books from the back seat of my car, climbed a flight of stairs, and entered the office area where I knew the pastor's study was. True, I was a little early moving, but George Ivy, the pastor I was following, had moved out of the pastor's study and I felt it would be all right to move in some books. On entering the office area I began meeting the secretarial staff upon whom I knew I would lean so heavily in the years to come. I looked into the office of the treasurer and asked in jest: "How was the offering Sunday? " Ruth Matthews looked up to see a stranger standing in her doorway and asking a question she was not sure she should answer. "And who are you?" she asked in a tone which meant, What business is that of yours? I replied timidly, "I'm your new pastor." From that time on thru the three years and nine months I served as pastor of that splendid church, she was my loyal supporter and a very efficient treasurer.

First Church, Ft. Smith, had been the leading United Methodist Church in the North Arkansas conference for many years. It had the largest membership and the largest Sunday School. It had three S.S. classes, each with a larger average attendance than many rural churches had in worship. Dr. Fred Roebuck, who had been the pastor for more than 20 years, knew the importance of a strong Sunday School and had worked very hard to make First Church's Sunday School the strongest in the state. Pastors who followed him continued this emphasis, so I inherited a great Sunday School.

Dr. Roebuck lived in Ft. Smith and attended First Church where he had been the pastor for so long that many members could not remember another pastor. I had heard that he might "get in the way" of pastors who followed him, but I did not find this to be the case. He supported my ministry in every possible way. Yes, he conducted many funerals, but I was glad for him to do this. If he hadn't, I think the church would have needed another associate pastor.

I preached in two worship services each Sunday, 8:30 A.M. and 11:00 A.M. I held the first service in Roebuck Chapel, obviously named for the beloved former pastor. The same order of worship was followed in both services. This period was before the popularity of "contemporary" worship services. The second service was broadcast over the radio. This presented no problem for me, because I had been on the radio at both Winfield, Little Rock, and Fayetteville Central. In all these places I concluded that a radio ministry was money well spent. It was a good way to keep touch with the church's "shutins", and it reached some people who never "darkened the door of a church."

First Church was ready for a building program. Lay leaders felt the need for better facilities for children and a larger fellowship hall/family life building. After some discussion, the church employed a fund-raising team from the Board of Global Ministries of the United Methodist Church. The campaign had a goal of one million dollars. As I recall, we raised it in pledges.

A children's building was constructed just back of the present educational section of the church. It would not only be used to house our children's division in Sunday School but also as a day care center for children.

Across the street we constructed the first phase of the family life center. That phase consisted of the main entrance, several rooms and a kitchen. Our plans included a large fellowship hall/sports arena to be constructed later. It was finished in the next year or two after I left.

Being the pastor during this building program was not an easy task, to put it mildly. I spent a good deal of time and energy trying to reconcile some differences of opinion on the "what" and "how" and "who" of the building program. I suppose this is about "par for the course", but I confess that this kind of golf was not my favorite sport. Nevertheless, the buildings were completed and consecrated while I was the pastor. I don't believe they completely retired the indebtedness when I retired.

The parsonage was a very nice two story house in a good neighborhood at the end of a cul de sac about ten minutes driving time south of the church and just down the street from the Roland Vernons.

We loved the Vernons. Roland, the father, was a heart surgeon. Nancy, the mother, was the church organist. They became our friends. Bill and I watched with delight their three children grow, baptized one of them, confirmed a couple of them, and, after I retired, read the marriage ceremony for Ann Elizabeth.

It was during this pastorate at lst Church, Ft. Smith, that the Cooper family suffered its first heart breaking incident. Chris was serving at Berryville. Dollie, his wife, was pregnant for the second time. A year or two earlier, she had given birth to a boy, named Matt after Dr. Matt Ellis. When Dollie's time came for birthing another boy, they hurried to the hospital at Eureka Springs. Things were not right, so Wesley was born but was injured at birth. He was transferred to Washington Regional Hospital where he lived only two weeks. Chris and Dollie suffered. We all suffered.

Sometime before Wesley died, Chris asked me to baptize Wesley. The family assembled in the hospital room. With my hand I dipped a little water from a basin and sprinkled some water on the tiny head. I left my hand on Wesley's head. Chris put his hand on top of mine as I said the words, "Wesley, I baptize you in the name of the Father, and the Son, and the Holy Spirit. Amen." Wesley had been born as a child of God. Now, in baptism, he was marked as a Christian child of God. That baptism did not "save" Wesley to eternal life. He would have been enfolded in the Father's arms without baptism. Still, baptism is the way the Christian community initiates persons into the Christian faith and is thought by some to be "necessary" and by others as "highly desirable". Wesley's "cremains' were buried in Fayetteville but later were moved to the family plot in Oak Grove Cemetery in Conway.

The second heart breaking incident revolved, again, around the Chris Coopers. Andee, a girl, their third child, was born with a cleft palate. This condition made it difficult for the baby to nurse. Dollie was persistent and patient, helping the baby do the almost impossible. The corrective surgeries began early and continued across the years, the latest surgery in 2006. The Ft. Smith surgeon, Dr. Cole Goodman, did a wonderful reconstructive job, and Andee has not suffered psychologically. Actually, she has become a beautiful, self-confident, outgoing person who graduated from Hendrix College. She is the only grandchild out of seven to graduate from my alma mater.

Dr. Vernon called me one day and said that a truck carrying "Shop Smiths" had wrecked and that they were selling these wood working machines on the spot for reduced prices. He wondered if I would be interested in buying one. I was, and did. That was the beginning of my woodworking hobby which was to become very important to me in my retirement years.

We brought with us to the Ft. Smith parsonage a dachshund named "Baron". He was a smart dog and we loved him, but he was now old and crippled. We were sad when he died, but replaced him with another dog named Snipper who loved to run down the street to see the Vernon's dog. Sadly, a car in Conway killed him while we were working on our retirement house. However, we got another one, black this time, named Trapper. We often called him "digger" because he was a tireless maker of holes in the ground. The last thing I did before moving into retirement was to fill the holes in the back yard, a hazard to life and limb.

Not only did First Church have an outstanding Sunday School, it had a wonderful music program under the direction of Edna Earls Massey, a dedicated musician and former public school teacher. The choir was large and produced music that "lifted" the congregation and me. Nancy Vernon, as I have said, was the splendid organist who gave herself without tiring, or so it seemed. She had the help of "husband" (the name she gave her husband Rowland) and a great organ.

Some unusual things happened to me as I moved thru my ministry in this great church. One day while climbing up the many front steps to the sanctuary, I noticed honey bees flying around an eve above a column. When I reported this, they told me that the bees had been there for several years, that they had studied how to eradicate them, but that they had reached no conclusion. The rationale: if the bees were killed by fumigation, the honey would run down into the sanctuary. To tear out the structure where the bees lived would be costly. The best solution seemed to be: leave them alone. I visited the church some 20 years later and found that the bees were still there—confirmed United Methodist honey bees, no doubt.

Once, in the middle of the night, the telephone's ringing awakened me. Lifting the receiver and sleepily muttering "hello", I heard a muffled voice. Perhaps my caller was attempting to disguise his voice:

"Preacher, give me one good reason why I should not take my own life. I have cut a vein in my wrist and I am sitting here watching my life ooze out." He paused. I almost fell out of bed. My mind whirled as best it could with sleep all over it, but I managed to say,

"Well, if I am to talk with you about this, you will first have to stop the bleeding." He must have followed my instruction, for we continued our conversation for a long time, maybe an hour or more. I do not know how long it takes for a person to bleed to death from a cut wrist. In any event we continued visiting. I can't remember what I said to him, but I remember thinking afterwards how inept I was in dealing with such a problem. I kept thinking of things I should have said to him and watching the papers for news of a suicide. I never saw the story I was afraid I would see.

I had a problem at First Church my last year as pastor. I wanted to raise the salaries of the staff to a certain level, but we had not received the pledges to justify this additional expense. The Administration Board was firm in its position that unless our pledges covered the raises, they would not give them. I asked the Board to give us more time for pledges to be received. The problem was intensified by the belief of some board members that I was pushing the raises to raise my own salary. Before God, that was not my motivation, and I tried to explain that to the Board. However, after the confrontation I know I became intransigent. It became a matter of pride; i.e., who could win the struggle? As I look back upon this, I know I was wrong in being so stubborn about the raises for the staff.

My inability to "go with the flow" of things made it hard to concentrate on my work and interrupted my sleep. Finally, I decided that I should retire that coming June 1984. I was 65 years of age, had already signed up for Medicare, and had served the conference for 40 years plus. I went to Bishop Hicks, explained the situation, and said, "Bishop, I want to retire." He said, "It looks like they won't let you be the pastor. I could move you to a good church, if you decide not to retire." If he had said, "to a district," I might have changed my mind about retiring. Bishop Galloway had always said to me, "When you are preparing to retire, go on a district, serve your time, and retire in style."

On returning from the bishop's office, I informed my district superintendent, Wayne Jarvis, of my intention to announce my retirement on the following Sunday. He said that he wanted to be present—and was. Wayne was a good friend who had supported me for bishop.

To underline my contention that I was not pulling for a raise in salary when I stood for the staff raises, I refused to accept the raise that they gave me. This rocked along for a couple of months. Our business manager, Tom Clark, came to me to say that the bishop had instructed him to pay me the salary that had been set. My stubborn reaction: "I will give the raise back to the church in one way or another." I did, and I believe I furnished Tom with a listing of the extra money I contributed. As I see it now, it was time to retire, if I couldn't handle matters better than I had been handling them.

One joy of being the pastor of First Church was the privilege of having my Duke room mate and his wife as members—Byron and Linda Cravens. They lived across the Arkansas River in Oklahoma, but not so far that they could not attend the church in Ft. Smith regularly. In the years I was the pastor, we had many happy times together.

Of course, in an old church like First, there were many shut-in members to be visited, many more than one pastor could handle. I worked out a plan which gave every "shut-in" on the list at least one visit each quarter from one of the staff, and that included at least one visit each year from the senior pastor. To accomplish this, we divided the list of "shut-ins" into four parts and rotated the visitors. I think this was the best approach to "shut-in" visiting that I had practiced in my years as a pastor. I visited my list religiously each quarter. From the many comments we received, I conclude that this was a system that worked. As I left this church for retirement, some significant monetary gifts to the Coopers came from "shut-ins". Not only do I appreciate the money, but I am grateful that some of it came from those who never were able to attend a worship service while I was the pastor.

Another project which I initiated was "Dial-a-Prayer". The church paid for a dedicated phone line which connected to a machine in my office on which I recorded prayers. I changed the prayers two or three times a week. A person could call any time of day or night and hear a prayer. I received many positive comments on this program, and people used it. One person said that she could not have made it thru a certain difficult time in her life without this program. That's all the pay a person ever wants.

The eleven o'clock Sunday worship service was broadcast over a local radio station. I am remembering one particular "shut-in" who was a regular listener and never failed to express appreciation when I called upon her in my rounds. I am just human enough to enjoy such, and must confess that I enjoy such too much.

At the close of a worship service one Sunday morning, I was standing, as usual, at a door in the back of the sanctuary greeting the congregants as they departed. One prominent member shook my hand vigorously and said, "Pastor, that was a **surprisingly** good sermon this morning." 'Nuff said.

One Sunday morning as I was beginning my sermon, there was a disturbance in the back of the sanctuary. Someone was calling out to me, "Pastor, pastor!" I looked up and coming down the isle was a man with long white hair, dressed in the garb of an 18th century preacher, carrying a Bible. I recognized him immediately, "O, it's John Wesley! Brother Wesley, come up to this pulpit. Welcome! I am sure you have a word for us," I said. The man joined me in the pulpit and our conversation, scripted, of course, became the sermon for the morning. The secret of the coming of this layman who dressed as John Wesley had been well kept. Not even the associate pastor knew what was happening. I don't think he has forgiven me for keeping him in the dark. It was all a part of a Methodist bicentennial celebration.

I did not have an increase in church membership during my three years and nine months at First Church. The membership roll had not been purged in a long time; i.e., the "lost, strayed, or stolen" members had not been removed from the roll. It was time to bite the bullet. The *Journal* for 1983 shows that I removed 1267 members by Church Conference action. That is a formidable hurdle. On a scale of one to ten, I would rate my Ft. Smith pastorate as a five plus, and hope that others might rate it higher.

The time had arrived for packing the truck to move. We had moved before, but this move was different. We were not going to another parsonage; we were moving into our own house, a completely new and exciting experience. On the morning I was packing the rented trailer, two helpers arrived. One was a psychiatrist and the other was Rowland, the heart surgeon. As they started to move our "stuff" into the truck, I remarked to them: "You can't get the kind of help these days that you used to."

While in Fayetteville, Bill and I had purchased a house in Conway, almost "sight unseen", as an investment and possible retirement home. We were so glad we had this place to move into as we began to plan our retirement. We had used part of the house as our "motel" when we had to be in central Arkansas. The rest of the house had been rented, part of the time to my brother, John, and his new wife, Pattie. Our boys had used the back apartment as they attended Hendrix College. Now this house would become our retirement home. It was well located, just across the street from Galloway Hall of Hendrix College. We had the house remodeled and a garage added.

There was a wild cherry tree right where they would build the garage. Since I had become interested in woodworking, I asked the contractor to have the tree cut into lumber. I later made several pieces of furniture out of this cherry lumber.

They held the Annual Conference at which I would retire, after 40 and a half years of service, in the Hendrix Staples Auditorium. It was June of 1984. I had joined the conference in November of 1943. On the morning when the retirement program was "the order of the day", Bill and I joined the other retirees and spouses on the stage of the auditorium. Those of us retiring that day represented many years of service to the conference, and, hopefully to the Kingdom. It is the custom of the North Arkansas Conference to give each retiree a chance to say a "word". I don't remember much of what I said and did not keep a copy, if indeed I had written my speech. I am sure I said something about my debt to Bill for all her encouragement and support in my work. And I tried to express my thanks to the conference for its support of me when I was being considered for the office of bishop and for giving me many places of service in the conference. I didn't take much time, but when I concluded my little speech I had the surprise of my life. Jim Beal, sitting on the front row of the auditorium, rose from his seat clapping vigorously. Then the whole conference gave me a "standing ovation". I know in my heart I did not deserve this, but I greatly appreciated it. I had not seen this done before. I was high.

The closing hymn was "Rock of Ages". My 40 years of service was uppermost in my mind. Surely, I thought, those years must have earned me a place in God's kingdom. Just then the singing congregation came to the words: "In my hand no price I bring, simply to the cross I cling." That brought my feet to the ground once again. I knew in my head that I could not give enough service to God's work to deserve a place beside Him. Now I think I was beginning to know it with my heart. GOD'S GRACE. That is really all I have going for me.

17

On Staff at Last

Our choice of Conway as the town in which we would spend our retirement years was not hard to make. We had a house in Conway. Conway was in the center of the state, so Chris, our preacher son, would always be just a few hours away, wherever the bishop sent him. Hendrix College was there. We had served First Church, Conway for ten years and had many friends there. Moreover, an anonymous donor had made it possible for Hendrix College to pay my salary as a part-time employee, something for which I had hoped. It was not that we needed the money to survive in retirement, although Bill thought we would starve. I just needed something to enable me to "come down" from the "high" I had been experiencing as an active minister of the gospel. The thought of not being in the big middle of things was sometimes very depressing. I fought this depression by working for Hendrix and doing woodworking.

The cherry lumber which I mentioned in the last chapter was now dried and ready for use, so I began to make pieces of furniture. Since the parsonages in which we had lived all furnished, we had not accumulated enough furniture of our own to furnish our retirement home. Woodworking was great fun, something new, challenging, and practical. Moreover, it kept my mind occupied, kept me "out of the pool hall", so to speak. I could not be depressed for long while working on the cabriole legs of a coffee table, for example.

Among the many pieces of furniture I made are these: coffee table, end tables and lamps for the couch, a game table, a revolving book case, computer table and matching printer table, assorted book cases, kitchen table, headboards for beds, bed side tables, entertainment center, butcher top table, stool, magazine racks, tea table, sofa table, side board. When I filled our house, I started making furniture for the kids and grand kids. For example, I made "hope" chests for my three grand-daughters, bookcases, gun rack, computer table, and armoire for my grand-sons, etc. Not all of these items were made of cherry, I say in passing. While we lived on Winfield Street, across from Hendrix's Galloway Hall, my shop was in the garage. When we moved to Sandstone Street, I had a separate shop. The ShopSmith to which Roland Vernon had directed me was the basic tool. It was a combination tool that sawed, bored, sanded, and was also a lathe.

I have included this paragraph on woodworking because it has been very important to the achievement of peace and happiness in my retirement, Moreover, I wanted my grands to see it.

Another hobby in retirement has been the computer. My brother, John, and my son, Chris, are both experts in this field and have dragged me into the computer age. I, in turn, have attempted to bring Bill along with me, but have had little success, she says.

Since my preaching/teaching did not end when I retired, I found the computer to be a very useful tool. I have remarked, "If I had had a computer while I was having to write a sermon every week, I might have written a good one now and then." At least, it would have been easier.

My woodworking and computer came together when I put the contents of several woodworking magazines into a data base. Now, when I want a plan for something, I go to my computer first and do a search. The computer spits out the plans with the names of the magazines, the date, and the page where the plans are to be found. I go to my files of magazines, drag out the proper magazine and date, and voila!

Someone from somewhere in my past contributed money for three or four years to Hendrix College to pay my part-time salary. I am heavily indebted to this anonymous donor. Jon Guthrie was the go-between. Dr. Joe Hatcher, president of the college, asked me to work with Rev.Jon Guthrie, college chaplain, and Dr. Jay McDaniel, religion professor and director of the Steel Center. The college refurbished an office for me in the Religion Building. At last, I was a staff member of the college, although part time. Dr. Ellis was happy.

My responsibilities with Jon Guthrie: work with the pre-theological students, help the Hendrix Christian Association plan the student worship services, etc. My work with the Steel Center: securing speakers for the several Steel Center events held each year.

One year, we had secured Senator Dale Bumpers to be our guest lecturer. Dr. McDaniel had asked me to introduce the Senator. I knew him. He had been kind enough to say a complimentary word about me, in a little brochure which had been distributed, plugging my election to the episcopacy. The time arrived and I rose to do the introduction of this well-known senator "who needed no introduction". I said, "I have heard that the length of the introduction of a speaker should be in an inverse proportion to the popularity of the speaker. I am pleased to introduce Senator Dale Bumpers." He was a little shaken by the brevity of my remarks, laughed and said, "Joel, that is the shortest introduction I have ever received."

Dr. McDaniel and I had wanted to get Dr. Martin Marty as one of our speakers. I wrote to him and gave the invitation. He wrote back, regretting. However, I did not want to give up and wrote him again. I reminded him of the lady in the Scriptures who got her wish because of her "importunity". He accepted my second invitation.

Dr. Albert Outler had been one of my professors in Duke Divinity School. He had spoken in First UMC, Conway while I was the pastor there, and I had visited with him when attending the Pastors' School at Perkins School of Theolog in Dallas. I invited him to be one of our speakers. He arrived after a harrowing experience. His plane was late. I waited in the Little Rock airport with increasing anxiety. The airport officials told me that his plane had to return to the Dallas airport. When he finally arrived, he said that soon after takeoff from the Dallas airport, his plane had run into a flight of geese. One or two of the geese had broken thru the glass surrounding the cockpit. Blood, glass, goose flesh, and feathers spattered the pilots, making it necessary for the plane to return to the airport. Dr. Outler appeared shaken as he told of the experience, but who wouldn't be?

Dr. Albert Outler is one of the teachers who helped form my theology, one to whom I owe more than I can repay, one who, to this day, looks over my shoulder as I write sermons asking: "Are you sure about that? Have you presented the idea clearly? Are you willing to stand by your words thru thick or thin?" After his death, I wrote Mrs. Outler telling of this "kibitzing" and expressing my appreciation for all the good doctor had meant to me and to Christendom.

This brilliant teacher and dedicated churchman was a Protestant representative to the Second Vatican Council. His knowledge of the Roman Catholic Church constantly amazed the Council members. He became so very well known that this story circulated: One morning Pope John Paul was about to open the council meeting. He looked to his left and then to his right and asked, "Where's Albert?"

One of my responsibilities at Hendrix was the planning of the Memorial Service on the Sunday of Alumni Weekend. I wanted to use, as a part of the service, the Navy Tune and the recurring words, "Lord God of hosts be with us yet, lest we forget…." I picked up some words from another hymn, metricized them, and wrote an extra stanza, We used this arrangement in the service. I feel greatly honored that Hendrix some fifteen or more years later is still using this arrangement.

After a couple of years working with the Steel Center and the Chaplain's Office, they named me director of Church Relations. My job was to keep the church and their pastors informed and happy about the work of Hendrix, a formidable task. Moreover, my work began to include money raising. Hendrix was in a capital funds campaign and they gave me the responsibility for raising funds for new seating in Staples Auditorium. The names of the donors to this project are listed on a plaque in the rear of Staples Auditorium.

Those days at Hendrix were happy days. I know now that I could have been happy spending my career as an employee of Hendrix, but the pastoral ministry was where I think God wanted me to be.

It was during those days that I received a call from the bishop to take on a special work for the conference. The United Methodist Church, the Presbyterian Church, the Episcopal Church, and the Disciples of Christ Church had been experimenting with a Cooperative Ministry in a new development known as Maumelle. The town was just north of the Arkansas River and west of North Little Rock. For perhaps twenty years the judicatories involved had given support to this ministry, financial and ministerial. The cut off date had arrived and the church had not grown enough to support itself without the help of the judicatories. What to do? The leaders of the participating judicatories met and came to the conclusion that the cooperative ministry must become a denominational entity.

They agreed that someone should be appointed as the pastor of the church while it decided what denomination it would be. I do not know just how I was picked for this job. Maybe because I was retired, lived close, and could do the job with no, or little, remuneration. In any event I was sent to Maumelle.

I preached every Sunday and tried to prepare the members for the vote that they would take. I tried not to push too hard for the church to become United Methodist.

Holy Communion was an interesting challenge. Episcopalians use wine; the other denominations involved used grape juice. We passed two cups. I could never tell by looking which was which, wine or grape juice. Bill got the wrong cup one morning. She said that it was good, but it was not her first time to have wine at Holy Communion. She drank wine in the Church of England which John Wesley attended while he was in the university.

We took the vote, and since there were more United Methodists in the Cooperative Ministry than any other denomination, the members decided to be a United Methodist Church. On the Sunday when we organized the First United Methodist Church of Maumelle, Dr. George Martin, District Superintendent, and I had the people stand who would like to become United Methodists. Most of the people in the congregation stood. That day we received 100 charter members into the new church, the most members I had ever received in a single service. Maumelle First is now a thriving church of 800 members with a beautiful and spacious sanctuary and educational facility.

After Maumelle became a United Methodist Church, the congregation began to grow. The idea of a Cooperative Ministry was a good one, but I think that the United Methodist sign in front of the church was more easily understood than "Maumelle Cooperative Ministries".

I was still working for Hendrix during the Maumelle episode. After completing five years on "staff" at Hendrix, I retired again. It was 1989.

18

"My Son! O My Son!"

On hearing of the death of his son, King David was inconsolable and cried out again and again, "O my son, Absalom, my son, my son Absalom. Would I had died instead of you, O Absalom, my son, my son!"

I knew that I would write this chapter sometime, but I dreaded it. I know that trying to put into writing the experiences surrounding the death of our son, Paul, will bring to the surface again the absolutely devastating emotions which rolled over us like a tsunami, which, to this day, makes me shudder at times.

Paul, the son who was born in Mt. Home, Arkansas, had graduated from Hendrix and had finished his PhD in statistics at Florida State. He had married Anita Dawson during his last year at Hendrix. They had two boys, John and Charlie, but Paul finished his schooling before they began their family. He worked a year or two at Fayetteville, then moved to TVA in Chattanooga, and finally to Ft. Huachuca in Sierra Vista, Arizona, to work for a company with government contracts in the field of communications. That is about all I can say about Paul's work, for it was classified. He did say once that his work would have civilian benefits. But what he did is not known to this day. It must have been very important, for officials of his company came to his house shortly after his death to check his computer for any information that must be kept secret.

The Paul Cooper family was active in the United Methodist Church of Sierra Vista. Anita taught special children's classes at the fort. All was going well for them, until ...

Our telephone rang. It was Anita who said, "Are you sitting down? I have bad news. Paul has Hodgkins Disease. He found lumps in his neck and shoulder. As you may know, it is more treatable than some cancers. There is a very good cancer center in Tucson. Paul will have to have surgery to remove his spleen, This is a normal first procedure for the treatment of Hodgkins. And then he will have radiation."

She paused for breath. I didn't know what to say to her, but I think I started asking questions like: "When did he first notice the lumps? When and where will he have the surgery? Do you want us to come out there?"—questions like that. My chest was about to explode. I do not cry. They tell me that people who do not shed tears on the outside actually cry on the inside. I don't know about that, but something inside was building up a terrible pressure. We finally concluded our conversation with the understanding that Anita would call us after the surgery.

Anita called and said, "Paul came thru the surgery ok. He now will go to Tucson for radiation. I don't feel that I can leave my work to do this, so it would be very helpful if you could come out here and drive Paul back and forth to take his treatments."

Of course, we would go. It's about 1200 miles from Conway to Sierra Vista, two days of hard driving. I had never been to that section of the country before. Bill had visited California as a girl. We decided to take the southern route, i.e., down to Dallas and on west. We spend the first night somewhere on the plains of Texas and drove across New Mexico and into Sierra Vista late the next day. There were moments when we enjoyed the scenery. It was new country for us and beautiful in its own way. But the reason for the trip was never out of our minds.

Paul and I talked on those first trips to Tucson for his treatments, but after awhile we listened to audio books as we rode back and forth. If it had not been for the seriousness of Paul's problem, we would have enjoyed our visit very much. Furthermore, never before had we been able to spend so much time with John and Charlie, our grands.

When Paul had finished the radiation treatments, Bill and I packed up and headed back to Conway. I think we were gone about a month. Paul seemed to be progressing about on schedule.

Paul and his family were able to visit us in Conway that summer. Although Paul was still weak, he was able to help us move from our house on Winfield to our new house on Sandstone. We had a good visit, but a bit hectic.

It must have been about a year before our telephone rang again. It was Anita. She said: "Paul's Hodgkins has returned." Bill and I decided that she would go to Sierra Vista to help while Paul recovered from a second surgery and began his chemo treatments. She stayed about two weeks.

Paul was making normal progress. After a few months, we visited the Sierra Vista Coopers again. It was during this visit that we decided to take the long way home and to take John and Charlie with us. We visited the Grand Canyon. What a marvel! We spent the Saturday night before July 4 in Salt Lake City, enjoyed a fireworks celebration, and that night and got caught in an awful traffic jam. The next morning, July 4, a Sunday, we went to the Mormon Tabernacle, heard the choir in a rehearsal and then the world wide broadcast. The choir's program that day was completely patriotic. Tremendous experience! Goose pimpling!

From Salt Lake City, we traveled on to Wyoming and Yellowstone National Park. We saw "Old Faithful" send her steaming water high into the air, and right on schedule. We drove across the park to Mt. Rushmore and then home, making sure we avoided the flooding Missouri River.

Shortly after arriving back in Conway from this wonderful trip with John and Charlie, we put them on the plane to go back to Sierra Vista. The telephone rang again. It was Anita who said, "Paul has been taken to the hospital in Tucson. He has pneumonia." We knew this was bad news, for the chemo treatments had knocked out Paul's immune system. This time we did not drive. We boarded the plane in Little Rock and arrived in Tucson sometime in the night, and went directly to the hospital.

Paul was very pleased to see us but because of the ventilator, he was not able to talk to us. He wrote many notes. We were terribly afraid. Days passed. They discouraged us one day and encouraged us the next. Once, while I was visiting and Paul was not hooked to the ventilator, he said to me, "Dad, I am scared." All I could think of at the moment was, "I understand." I did not know it at the time, but those words were his last words to me. I thought then and still think: I am a minister. Surely there is something more that I could have said. It haunts me. To describe in more detail this experience of losing Paul is more than I can do at this time.

I was in the delivery room when Paul was born; I was in his hospital room when he died. In between this moment of supreme joy and this moment of wrenching grief, there lived a wonderful boy and man. He was a believer in Jesus Christ, a churchman, a person with a highly-developed sense of right and wrong, a family man, highly intelligent, devoted to his work, a fisherman, and a woodworker. Bill and I were, and are, so very proud of him!

Paul's death was indescribably difficult to accept. We thought the usual "what ifs". We wondered if the doctors did everything they could have done. Did we do all we could do? We were grief stricken and angry at the same time. I don't think we were angry at God, just angry. And the usual "Why, God?" kept playing over and over again in our minds. Paul's death did not make sense to us. He was too young, too useful, too good. I had preached so many times about the death of loved ones, but this was something different. It was my son, OUR son. Could I put into practice what I had preached? Did I really believe that God is love? Why would He permit such a tragedy, if He is all loving. Is it because He is not in control of everything? I have preached on the omnipotence of God. It is one thing to deal in theory with the problem of suffering and death, and it is quite another thing to be personally involved as we now were.

Here is what I hang onto: I believe in God; I cannot give that up or all is lost. If I believe He is a God of love, and Paul dies, then I must believe that God somehow makes sense of what does not makes sense to me. I do not have to know how God does this, but I **do** have to believe that He does make sense of it. I will never know the mind of God, not until that day when I stand before Him, but I am going to live my life on the assumption that God makes sense of what has happened, i.e., that ultimately what has happened fits somehow into God's grand scheme of things, what he is doing thru the human race. I think that our God-given freedom is somehow tied into all this, but this is a tangle about which I know very little. Living with these thoughts is part of what I mean by living by faith.

For many years, when the family gets together, we sing the blessing at our meals. It is a little chorus which I had learned on Mt. Sequoyah. It goes: "O, the Lord's been good to me, and so I thank the Lord for giving me the things I need, the sun, and the rain, and the apple-seed. The Lord's been good to me."

Marc, Chris, Clay and I had the Service of Committal for Paul. We had agreed that we would conclude the service by singing the "Johnny Apple-seed Song". That would be our way of saying that in spite of Paul's death, we still held on to God "from whom all blessings flow". It was hard; we barely managed it. Somehow we were strengthened to sing: "O, the Lord's been good to me...."

19

"Grace Upon Grace"

Five men sat at a table in Worthen Bank in Conway drinking coffee, but coffee was not their reason for being together. Bishop Wilke had called the meeting to discuss the establishment of a new United Methodist Church in western Conway. Present at the meeting: Bishop Wilke; Herschell McClurkin, Conway district superintendent; Marlin Jackson, president of the bank; Jerry Rea, a lay member of Wesley UMC; and yours truly. After considerable discussion, Bishop Wilke looked across the table at me and asked, "Joel, will you start this new church?" I answered, "I'll ask my wife." The bishop took that answer to be "yes", as indeed I meant it to be. I took his question to be his official appointment of me as the organizing pastor.

Things were about to come full circle. Twenty-five years ago, as I preached my last sermon at Conway First Methodist, I said that a new church ought to be organized in Conway. I did not know then that I would be the one to do what I had suggested. I should have remembered the well-known advice, "Never make a suggestion, if you do not want to be the chair of the committee."

This meeting was not the first time that a new church in Conway had been considered. Herschell McClurkin, district superintendent, had formed a committee and had asked me to chair its meetings. The committee had met several times over the last months, so we were "several miles down the road" when Bishop Wilke gave the official green light.

We started at zero. We had no money and no one committed to help in the project. I take that back. We had Mardell McClurkin, talented and vivacious wife of the district superintendent, who, from the very first gave untold hours helping in every way she could. My first step was to ask the Administrative Boards of the United Methodist Churches in Conway for permission to write to the members of the churches seeking help in establishing a new church in western Conway. When permission was granted, I wrote letters in June of 1992, asking for prayers, work, members, and money. Several thousand dollars were pledged. Perhaps a dozen persons showed a willingness to do work, and maybe a half dozen indicated a willingness to become charter members. Among these were Bill Farris and his wife Pearl.

The next step was a telephone survey to discover who might be interested in the new church. I called upon the few persons who had agreed to work for the establishment of the church. Hendrix College gave us the use of the telephones in the Raney building, after class hours, of course. The telephone committee made thousands of calls, nearly every family with a telephone in Conway. We asked those whom we called a simple question, "Would you be interested in seeing a new United Methodist Church established in western Conway." Several hundred families showed an interest, and became the start of our mailing list.

Meanwhile, we had secured the permission of the Wesley Foundation, on the UCA campus, to hold our morning worship services in its chapel.

We set the time for our first worship meeting for a Sunday afternoon so that members of other United Methodist Churches in the city could attend. About 150 persons attended this first service. The next Sunday we started worship at 11 A. M. and our attendance was about 40.

For several months "new church" met in the Wesley Foundation Chapel. In June the bishop appointed me to be the pastor of "New Church Conway". After considerable debate, the persons attending decided to call the church "Grace United Methodist".

During these months, we were collecting money to buy property. The Annual Conference gave a sizeable amount to the new church project. We searched for the property that would be "just right" and finally found it on Hogan Road, a street running north and south in the far western part of the city. Bill Farris was instrumental in locating and making the deal for the property.

My wife, Bill, was with me every step of the way, praying, teaching SS, helping to clean the building, making visits and phone calls, helping with mailings and bulletin preparation. I could not have done this work without her.

She had been keeping the children, who were too small to enjoy the worship service, in a room next to the chapel. Several little ones had not experienced Sunday School and she was teaching some basics, among these, The Lord's Prayer. One Sunday she allowed the children to crack the door and listen to the worship. One little fellow listened intently and then remarked in glee, "Listen, they are saying what you "teached" us." They needed a lot of teaching.

Finally, the new church, now named GraceUMC was constituted and the list of charter members recorded.

It was during this time that our son, Paul, fell ill and died.

Early in the planning stage of Grace UMC, I had visited with Rev. Bob Crossman, associate pastor of lst UMC, Conway. I remembered saying, "Bob, I will get this new church started and then I will turn it over to you." We both laughed because we knew that there was "many a slip twixt the cup and the lip." But, that it did happen just that way seems to support the idea that this was what God wanted to happen.

Soon after they had appointed Bob to Grace as pastor, the congregation outgrew its meeting place. Hendrix College came to the rescue again, letting Grace have worship space in a lecture room of the Mills Center and making available other space for Sunday School classes. Everything necessary for the church to operate was moved in every Sunday morning and out when the service was concluded. It was tough, but the church grew.

We had collected about enough money to pay for the property. Now, we had to begin raising money for the new building.

The first unit of Grace Church was completed: a sanctuary, offices, and Sunday School rooms. The money for the debt payments kept coming in. The church grew. They constructed another unit. The church continued to grow. It's membership now is almost 800.

Bill and I continued to attend Grace after Bob became the pastor. Bill had been a charter member. I, of course, was a member of the conference. While it may not always be the best policy for a founding pastor to stay in the church after the new pastor arrives, I did not feel uneasy, nor did Bob. He treated me with the utmost courtesy, giving me much more credit than I deserved in the establishment of the church.

Bill and I stayed and worked in Grace until Chris moved to Morrilton in 2000. It was then that Bill said, "I have never had my son as pastor. I want us to go to Morrilton." We did. Bill was a member there until Chris moved six years later to Blytheville. Then Bill joined First UMC, Conway for the fifth time. Some wag remarked, "Maybe she will get it right this time."

The Sunday morning that Bill joined First Church, the hymn before the sermon was "Amazing Grace". The words of the third stanza jumped out at me; "Through many dangers, toils, and snares, I have already come; 'tis grace hath brought me safe thus far, and grace will lead me home." My mind raced. I thought of that Sunday long ago when I first became pastor of this church, how I knelt at that communion rail, just ten feet away from where I was sitting now. I looked at the very spot where I knelt, and remembered how I had prayed that God would not let me fall flat on my face as I tried to preach to this congregation. My mind jumped to Vanndale, my first charge, to Mt. Home and the larger parish, to Conway and a building program, to Winfield and the racial problems, to Fayetteville and the fire, to Ft. Smith and the closing years of my ministry. And I thought of those years since retirement. Then I thought, "what if I had been elected bishop? Would I have had the opportunity to be a part of the beginning of two new United Methodist Churches, Maumelle and Grace? Probably not." I know I was supposed to listen to the sermon, but my mind was racing from one appointment to another, the good times and the bad. Suddenly we were standing and singing the closing hymn. I tried but I could not sing. Instead of singing my fingers traced the words in the hymn book, page 361: "Not the labors of my hands can fulfill the law's demands; could my zeal no respite know, could my tears forever flow, all for sin could not atone; thou must save, and thou alone." We moved to the third stanza: "In my hand no price I bring, simply to the cross I cling."

Epilogue

Since my retirement from the itinerant ministry in 1984, our family has suffered thru the deaths of five members. I have already mentioned the deaths of my mother and our son, Paul. Chris' wife, Dollie, died of pancreatic cancer after a painful and lingering illness. My sister, Nestel Wilkinson, died of the same disease on Christmas Day, just three weeks later. John Cooper, grandson, and son of Paul and Anita Cooper, was killed in an automobile accident just before he was to graduate from high school. It is hard, but the family continues to sing, sometimes in tears, the little chorus "O, the Lord's been good to me, and so I thank the Lord...."

But our spirits have been lifted by two marriages. Paul's widow, Anita, married Joe Ladensack, a former Roman Catholic priest. Chris married Kathy Thompson, a school teacher and his high school class mate whom I had baptized as an infant.

My wife, Bill, and I have reached that time in life when, as some wag said, we "just sit and hold hands—she holds hers and I hold mine." Mercy! We still feel the call of Christ to be "up and at 'em", and try, at times. But, as never before, we know we are saved by God's grace shown in Christ Jesus, and by nothing else. "No price I bring."

978-0-595-48427-0
0-595-48427-1